Champagne Music

Champagne Music

The Lawrence Welk Show

by

COYNE STEVEN SANDERS

and

GINNY WEISSMAN

ST. MARTIN'S PRESS/NEW YORK

Design by Jacques Chazaud

Library of Congress Cataloging in Publication Data

Sanders, Coyne Steven.
Champagne music.

1. Lawrence Welk Show (Television program)
2. Welk, Lawrence, 1904–   . 3. Musicians—
United States—Biography.   I. Weissman, Ginny.
II. Title.
ML422.W33S26   1985   785.4'1'0924 [B]
85–11881
ISBN 0–312–12827–4

First Edition

10 9 8 7 6 5 4 3 2 1

To Lawrence Welk
and every member
past and present
of his
Musical Family,
and to everyone who loves
Champagne Music

Contents

Acknowledgments   *ix*

Foreword   *xi*

Champagne Music   *1*

Bibliography   *141*

Index   *143*

Acknowledgments

The authors wish to thank the following people who freely gave of their time and memories: Dick Dale, Myron Floren, Cissy King, George Cates, Ralph Portner, Rudy Horvatich, Joe Rizzo, Roselle Friedland, Rose Weiss, Charles Koon, Mike Freedman, Eddie Holland, and Dick Connolly. We extend special thanks to Norma Zimmer, Bobby Burgess, Wally Stanard, Barbara Boylan Dixon, Charlotte Harris Buck, Jim Balden, Bob Ralston, Ron Bacon, Nick Pantelakis, and Kathy Lennon, who, in addition, made available to us photographs and other memorabilia from their private collections.

We express personal thanks to our resident interview transcriber, Richard Jordan; to Robert Osborne, Don Azars, John Graham, Ron O'Brien, Tom Klein, David Winters, Lynette Cimini, and Mike and Sara Matoin; and to our parents, Richard and Margaret O'Malley, and Josephine and Edwin Komos.

Thanks also to our incomparable agent, Dominick Abel, and our editor, Tom Dunne (who created this project), and his assistant, Pam Hoenig.

A special note of gratitude to three people who were instrumental in the preparation of this book, offering to us materials and resources inestimable in their value: George Thow (for generously providing us with many photos from the show's later years); Mark Zimmer (a one-man *Who's Who* on "The Lawrence Welk Show"); and photographer Don Keck, whose fine work seen in these pages presents a valuable record of "The Lawrence Welk Show"'s early years. Mr. Keck's remarkable collection of over fifty thousand photographs from the Welk show alone have truly made this book possible, and we offer him our sincere appreciation for his extraordinary generosity in making them available to us.

Foreword

I was a big Lawrence Welk fan, along with all my family, while I was growing up in Long Beach, California. I spent most every New Year's Eve in the early 1950s watching the Welk show on local TV, never thinking I'd be a part of the Musical Family one day.

To me, this book is like reading a personal family history. It has some inside information only the cast has ever talked about. What makes it different from the other books written about "The Lawrence Welk Show" is that the authors talked to people behind the scenes, some with the show more than twenty-five years, who had insightful and interesting observations.

This book is so well written and easy to read that you'll breeze right through it. You'll learn all kinds of new stories about the longest-running weekly musical show in television history.

—Bobby Burgess

Champagne Music

(Courtesy George Thow Collection)

There is no doubt that Lawrence Welk, his Champagne Music, and his Musical Family have secured a unique and lasting place in television history as well as in the hearts of the American public. Welk's impoverished beginnings as the sixth child of a dirt farmer in Strasburg, North Dakota, at first glance seems a most unlikely source for a show business phenomenon. Lawrence Welk offers this understatement of his accomplishments: "I'm a farm boy who got into the music business."

Yet it may well *be* Welk's humble but loving, disciplined upbringing that has given him such remarkable determination, respect for hard work, and strong religious and moral convictions. These qualities, together with Welk's unerring ability to please his audience and the genuine, deep admiration he has for the American public, explain the amazing love affair between Welk and his audience that has lasted well over thirty years—a truly remarkable achievement for a man who has only a fourth-grade education and who did not learn to speak English until the age of twenty-one.

Would anyone have gambled on the bet that this dirt-poor child with no social or economic advantages would one day become America's premier bandleader with a television cast of several dozen people and a top draw in concerts around the country, making him one of the wealthiest men in show business with an empire generating an estimated $25 million annually? The fact that Welk's climb was so seemingly unlikely has only further endeared him to the millions of fans who

(Courtesy George Thow Collection)

2

were uncommonly loyal to Welk and "The Lawrence Welk Show" for the several decades of its run.

Today, Lawrence Welk and his long-running program have become not only members of many a TV-watching family and a part of American show business lore, but also a television event that has made entertainment history.

No one could have predicted such future success for Lawrence, born on March 3, 1903, the sixth child of German immigrants Christina and Ludwig Welk. (Two more children would complete the family.) "They brought with them nothing but their prayer books, their high hopes and their utter belief in freedom and democracy," remembers Welk, who was born in the sod house his father built.

Lawrence and his parents quickly realized that he was ill-suited to farm life and instead discovered his real passion: music. Even as a young child, Lawrence had the unfocused sense that he stood apart from the rest of the family in his intense passion for music. Music was his "home," the one place Lawrence felt happy and secure, as he was certain he was "inferior" to his parents and siblings in every other way, considering himself, "the smallest, skinniest, homeliest member of the whole group."

In exchange for young Lawrence's remaining on the farm for four additional years, his father presented him with four hundred dollars to purchase a piano accordion. The seventeen-year-old further agreed to give his parents every penny he earned playing for dances and weddings. "I'll never forget the day the accordion arrived," recalls Welk fondly, "sparkling rhinestones and new-style piano keyboard. I started practicing like mad!"

In 1924, on his twenty-first birthday, Lawrence left the farm "dressed in my best and ready to tackle the world!" Years later, Welk summed up his early years on the farm by concluding that "in spite of the fact that our life was hard—very hard, with long work days that started at daybreak—I remember those years as very happy ones."

"Lawrence would tell us often, 'The Lord has given me the gift of the common man. I'm not musical. Boys, if you're musical, you'll lose your audience. The farmers come in from their hard day milking the cow and tending the crops and they want to put their feet up and drink beer and listen to the polkas.'"

—BOB RALSTON

The next few months were very difficult ones as Lawrence struggled to succeed in his new career. In the fall, Lawrence believed his luck had changed when he met an orchestra leader named Lincoln Boulds and joined his band when Boulds played a date in South Dakota while on a cross-country tour. Welk soon realized that joining the Lincoln Boulds Orchestra was an unfortunate move—Boulds was notorious for either conveniently "forgetting" to pay his musicians or being flat broke due to his own poor management. Eventually fed up with the situation, Welk quit, sadder but much wiser.

In the summer of 1925 Lawrence ventured to a lake resort in Iowa where he met itinerant showman George T. Kelly and his wife, Alma. The Kellys, along with another couple, comprised an act they called "The Peerless Entertainers." George was so taken with young Lawrence that he invited him to join their group as both accordionist and actor. Alma Kelly also took on the formidable task of teaching the twenty-one-year-old Lawrence how to speak and write English. Lawrence terminated his association with "The Peerless Entertainers" when George Kelly's alcoholism led to the premature ending of their road tour.

After performing as an accordion soloist for a time, Lawrence created a small orchestra. Initially, his band was composed of drums and the accordion; later, he added a saxophone and a piano. Soon gaining immense regional popularity, Lawrence and his small orchestra got their first real break in 1927 when radio station WNAX hired "Lawrence Welk and His Hotsy Totsy Boys—The Biggest Little Band in America," to play at the opening-day broadcast in Yankton, South Dakota. They were so successful that Welk and his musicians remained at WNAX for six years, in addition to the countless grueling one-night-stand engagements they played throughout the Midwest.

"I wish I could talk that way. It made him a millionaire."

—DICK DALE

It was during Lawrence's first year in Yankton that he met a pretty young student nurse named Fern Renner, who had aspirations of someday becoming a physician or medical researcher. Unlike most of the other young women in Yankton, who were quite taken with Welk and the other musicians,

Lawrence and Fern, still waltzing after all these years. (Courtesy Don Keck)

4

Fern had little interest in meeting the band or its leader, even though the members of the group had become established as local celebrities of sorts with a name value that extended over a four-hundred-mile radius.

Fern finally was convinced by the other girls to see Welk and his band perform. He spotted her in the audience and was immediately captivated. Her air of indifference was such a contrast to the usual star-struck adulation from the women in that town that Fern sparked curiosity in young Lawrence. Only after several weeks of persistence did he manage to talk Fern into a double date on the provision that she be returned home by 8:30 P.M. sharp. Then Lawrence even arranged to have minor surgery at the hospital where Fern worked as a student nurse so that he could be closer to her. This incident charmed Fern so much that their courtship began in earnest, and in 1931 the young couple decided to get married.

Lawrence proposed only because he now felt more secure, with bookings coming in steadily after his having played larger midwestern ballrooms and an eastern tour. Lawrence and Fern were married at 5:30 A.M. on April 19, 1931, in Sacred Heart Cathedral in Sioux City, Iowa. The ceremony was followed by a quick breakfast of coffee and doughnuts. The wedding was held at such an early hour because Lawrence and the band had to be on the road that morning to get to their next performance in another town, a pattern that was to be repeated over and over again throughout the early years of their marriage.

Mr. and Mrs. Lawrence Welk and the musicians later returned to Yankton, and Welk immediately booked a date in Dallas that proved to be a turning point for Welk both personally and professionally—Fern discovered that she was pregnant and Welk's musicians walked out on him, suddenly and without warning.

Stunned at the defection, Welk asked a band member for an explanation. "You're never gonna make it in the big time!" he said angrily. "You still bounce around like you're at a barn dance and you can't even speak English! So if you want to know the real reason I'm leaving, it's you. You're holding us back!" It was, Lawrence says, "the lowest moment of my lifetime."

Welk soon recovered his spirit, however, and out of that wreckage assembled a new group of musicians that, in short order, proved both more commercially and financially successful, and allowed for the addition of a second child (another daughter) to the Welk family.

On New Year's Eve 1938, Welk landed a twenty-week radio program on the Mutual Network that was broadcast from Pittsburgh's William Penn Hotel and provided the band's first national exposure. Immediately, fan mail poured in that praised Welk's musical sound as sparkling, light, effervescent, bubbly, and happy. The common thread of those letters gave birth to "Lawrence Welk and His Champagne Music Makers" and the introduction of their female vocalist, "The Champagne Lady."

In 1940, the Welk's third and last child—and only son—Lawrence Leroy Welk, Jr., was born. The icing on the cake for that year was an important booking at the Trianon Ballroom in Chicago that began as a twelve-week engagement and turned into nine years, with appearances divided between the Trianon and its sister dance hall, the Aragon Ballroom, also in Chicago.

In addition, Welk did twelve radio broadcasts a week from the Trianon heard over local radio station WGN. Fern was delighted that the family could live properly in one place and have a stable homelife. And as the children grew so did Welk's musical reputation, which gained stature through the 1940s.

Welk and his orchestra were based eleven months out of the year at the Trianon and toured cross-country during the remaining month. It was while appearing in St. Louis in 1949 that Welk hired a musician who would prove to be one of the most important and enduring people in his life—Myron Floren, whom Welk would describe as "the finest accordionist in the United States, if not the world." When Welk told the Trianon's manager about hiring Myron Floren, he became enraged and told Welk, "One accordion is bad enough, but two!" The first time Myron played with Welk's band the Trianon's manager sought out Welk at intermission, saying, "Welk, they tell me that the new accordionist plays better than you do!" to which Welk replied, "That's the only kind of musician I hire."

Seeing a roadside billboard advertising Miller High Life as "The Champagne of Bottled Beer" and making the connection with "Lawrence Welk and His Champagne Music Makers," Lawrence was inspired to pursue a meeting with Mr. Miller himself in Milwaukee to pitch the idea of Miller sponsoring Welk's band on a national radio show. He clinched the deal by offering to prominently feature the name of the product on the music stands and stage decorations. Welk also convincingly argued that the consumption of

Myron Floren, "The Accordion Man." (Courtesy Don Keck)

Miller High Life would rise wherever the band would appear. An agreement was quickly made.

Welk and his Champagne Music Makers were signed to a twenty-six-week contract for one broadcast weekly over the ABC Radio Network, either from the Trianon or from wherever they were appearing during their one-month coast-to-coast tour of the year. Welk hurriedly returned to Chicago to share the good news with his band, which had grown to well over a dozen members. The premiere broadcast emanated from New York on June 1, 1949. True to his agreement, Welk more often than not was able to convince each ballroom that broadcasted the show to have ample supplies of Miller High Life on hand—and usually, by intermission an unopened bottle of the brew could not be found.

The ABC radio program proved to be equally heady and intoxicating for Lawrence Welk and His Champagne Music Makers. The number of stations carrying the show ballooned from 38 to 105 and Miller High Life extended Welk's contract for another twenty-six weeks. The program, Welk recalls, "worked out beyond our wildest expectations."

It was at one of the Miller High Life broadcasts in Iowa that Lawrence Welk met singer-saxophonist Dick Dale, who would become one of the most enduring members of the Lawrence Welk Musical Family.

Dick Dale mugging during a "Top Tunes and New Talent" rehearsal, 1958. (Courtesy Wally Stanard)

A money dispute at the Trianon—management refused to consider any raise in salary during the entire ten years Welk played there—led Sam Lutz, Welk's manager, to arrange a West Coast tour in early 1951. After a succession of dates, Welk was booked for four weeks in May at the Aragon Ballroom in Santa Monica, California, to be followed by several other appearances. By this time, Welk had severed his association with Miller High Life and had ended his radio broadcasts, choosing instead to break into still-embryonic television.

Sam Lutz campaigned for local television station KTLA in Los Angeles to broadcast the Welk band from the Aragon, something the station had been doing for all the bands that played there. Unfortunately, diminished popularity of the KTLA remote broadcasts caused their cancellation just as Welk's band was set to appear at the Aragon. Lutz, however, was determined to get Lawrence Welk and his band on television.

Lutz was unsuccessful in reaching KTLA program director Klaus Landsberg despite innumerable telephone calls placed to Landsberg's office at the station. By chance, Lutz managed to get his home phone number, and when he called Landsberg himself answered.

"I was getting ready to go out to a dance and I had packed everything but a tie. I knew the guy next door was with the band so I went over and said, 'I'm your neighbor and I'm a musician, too, and I don't have a tie. Do you have a spare tie?' He said, 'Sure,' and that's how I met the band."

—DICK DALE

*"Wunnerful,
wunnerful!"*
(Courtesy
George Thow
Collection)

After initially rejecting Lutz's sales pitch, Landsberg softened. Welk's television appearance on KTLA would happen only if two important conditions were met: Welk would have only one chance and was to assume all band expenses, estimated at $300. Lutz quickly phoned Welk in Portland, Oregon, where he was performing. Lawrence immediately saw the great value of television exposure and gave Lutz the go-ahead, assuring him that he and his orchestra and Champagne Lady Roberta Linn would make their local television debut on KTLA on May 2, 1951, one day after opening at the Aragon Ballroom.

The live, remote broadcast from the Aragon followed the Humphrey Bogart/Lauren Bacall film *To Have and Have Not*. As programming in those days of television differed from the practices of today, the band remote was scheduled to begin whenever the film ended its broadcast and thus the program from the Aragon did not begin until 11:30 P.M.

The television broadcast did not vary from Welk's usual dance hall performance: The camera traveled across the bandstand and scanned the dancers as they moved under the Aragon's famous revolving chandelier. There had not even been a rehearsal.

Lawrence Welk was completely unaware of the impact of television until he went out to play golf the morning after the program. When more than twenty people approached Welk to tell him they had seen the broadcast the night before, it was only then that Welk realized the "tremendous potential of this powerful medium." Instantly, Lawrence Welk envisioned his own national television show.

"Welk was booked into the Aragon by MCA [a large and powerful talent agency] but after two weeks they wanted to book another band and kick Lawrence out because they would get a bigger commission. Had MCA been successful in ousting Lawrence he may never have been in television."

—RALPH PORTNER, announcer

That dream of a national television program proved to be possible and in fact was realized in a relatively short period of time. Welk was a smash at KTLA and the station quickly signed him to a long-term contract. And, unlike that first broadcast, KTLA and not Welk would pay the band expenses.

Welk embarked on a back-breaking schedule, playing the Aragon Ballroom nightly (including Sunday) until the early hours of the morning in addition to his live television show. Even now he was always unsure of his on-the-air demeanor and painfully sensitive about his broken-English delivery. Still, his program improved with each passing week and ratings climbed steadily.

The events leading up to Welk's landing a national television program seemed to fall so effortlessly into place that it further strengthened Sam Lutz's belief that the Champagne Music Makers were ready for the big time.

A woman who was an avid Welk fan was persistent enough to convince her husband to see Welk at the Aragon Ballroom; her husband, Bert Carter, happened to be well-placed with the Dodge Motor Company and was interested in acquiring a television show that would be sponsored by the Southern California Regional Dodge Dealers Association. He was in fact scouting talent with possible national television show potential. Bert Carter was so impressed with Welk and his Champagne Music Makers that his subsequent recommendation led to Welk being one of three final candidates for the Dodge-sponsored show. Welk's audition disc included a spoken message thanking Dodge for its consideration.

The day after Welk cut that recording, the Dodge dealers convened to decide which program to sponsor: Welk or one of his two competitors—popular singer Connie Haines and Xavier Cugat and His Orchestra. Lawrence Welk was the clear favorite and thus began the unusually warm association between Welk and the Dodge Motor Company that would last for nine years.

Another step closer to his goal: Welk's local program on KTLA would have an important national sponsor.

After a few years of enjoying great success at the Aragon Ballroom and with his KTLA television program, Welk was becoming more and more determined to get a network television series—and soon. With uncanny timing, prominent TV producer Don Fedderson walked into his office and confirmed Welk's own belief that national exposure was the next logical step. Welk was instantly impressed by Fedderson, who had launched Liberace into television stardom in addition to having produced the hit 1950s TV series "The Millionaire." Fedderson offered to represent Welk as his "television consultant and agent," to which Welk agreed. The first thing Fedderson did was to produce a short pilot film showcasing Welk and his Champagne Music.

Fedderson put together a first-rate promotional package and used it to convince Dodge's advertising agency in New York to sponsor the show nationally. It was so successful that Dodge bought the Welk series as a summer replacement for Danny Thomas's "Make Room for Daddy."

Welk was overjoyed at Fedderson's news, but when his elation subsided for a moment he thought of more practical matters. He told Fedderson they needed to find a handsome young TV announcer who could speak good English. Fedderson told him, "They don't want a handsome young TV announcer. They want you."

Welk got his first taste of how television can often be run by committee when he and his associates met with Dodge, the Grant Advertising Agency (Dodge being their client), and the ABC Network brass. At the start of the meeting, Welk gave a rundown of the premiere show. An executive from the Grant Agency, John Gaunt, then suggested some conceptual changes, explaining that in view of competing programs it might be wise to "spice it up a little." Welk, Sam Lutz, and Welk's champion at Dodge, Bert Carter, all blanched and quickly rose to Welk's defense as John Gaunt continued to speak of wanting big production numbers that would add excitement and glamour to the show.

Someone suggested adding a chorus line of girls and the others chimed in their approval. The idea of adding a comedian was also met favorably by all but the Welk contingent. Welk, in fact, was horrified as he watched his dream slip away, knowing that nothing in the world would make him put a line of girls or a comic on his show even if it meant the end of the deal with Dodge.

Spurred into action, Welk rose to his feet with great emotion—and conviction—and took the floor, proclaiming, "I want to do this show more than I can say. But, I'll give it up before I do it this way!" Welk triumphed. "The Lawrence Welk Show" would be done his way and his way only—a fact never to change over Lawrence Welk's entire tele-

vision career, which lasted nearly three decades.

"Our production staff has tried at various times to inject a little comedy into our show. After one such attempt, Lawrence scolded them, saying, 'You have to realize that our show is ninety-five percent music, and only fifteen percent comedy!'"

—MYRON FLOREN

The date was set for the first regularly scheduled taste of Champagne Music coast-to-coast: July 2, 1955. The program would air live from the West Coast at 6 P.M., and be seen later in the East. Welk had as his competition the quiz show "Two for the Money" and "It's Always Jan" (a situation comedy starring Janis Paige that lasted only one season) on CBS and "People Are Funny" and "Texaco Star Theater Starring Jimmy Durante" on NBC. Welk's lead-in was a ninety-minute country-western variety series called "Ozark Jubilee."

Early in 1955, Jack Minor, the vice president of the Grant Advertising Agency, fought network opposition to give "The Lawrence Welk Show" a chance. The president of ABC, Robert E. Kinter, thought Welk a "North Dakota cornball." Minor retaliated by threatening to pull "The Bert Parks Show" and "Make Room for Daddy"—which was the program Welk had replaced for the summer—if ABC did not relent. That pressure made the difference, and "The Lawrence Welk Show" was put on the ABC schedule, albeit with great reluctance.

Lawrence Welk's television family was composed of musicians and singers who had been with him from his days on the road and his Miller High Life stint; it included Myron Floren, Dick Dale, Rocky Rockwell, Jim

Proverbs on Learning

Ethel Kvalheim

• **Det er lettere å lære det en ikke trenger å vite.**
It is easier to learn that which you don't have to know.

• **Ingen er så klok at han ikke kan gjøre feil.**
No one is so smart that he cannot make a mistake.

• **Han som lite vet, glemmer lite.**
One who knows little has little to forget.

• **De dårligste bokene har de lengste titlene.**
The worst books have the longest titles.

• **Visdom kan en gjemme, men ikke dumhet.**
Wisdom you can hide, but not stupidity.

• **En god latter forlenger livet.**
A good laugh prolongs life.

...r Lon in an early broadcast.

Roberts, Larry Hooper, violinist-singer Alad...
din Pallante, violinist Bob Lido, pianist Tiny
Little, Jr., guitarist Buddy Merrill, the Sparklers Quartet, and musical director George
Cates. The one notable exception was that of
Champagne Lady Roberta Linn, who left in
1954 reportedly to capitalize on other offers
that resulted from her television exposure on

...ta lost the
...ision to
...Dick
...had
...re
on ...
joined...
to-coast...

11

Alice Lon was a vivacious, dark-haired woman with a warm, powerful voice. From a musically talented family, Alice debuted on a radio broadcast at the age of six and had her own program by the time she was ten. Her most recent and prominent exposure at that time was on the Chicago-based program "The Breakfast Club," with Don McNeill.

Lawrence Welk called Alice Lon "the perfect replacement" for Roberta Linn and she was an immediate hit with the Aragon Ballroom and KTLA audiences alike. Alice's enthusiasm and willingness to put in extra long hours of rehearsal with the band further endeared her to Welk and his Musical Family. Everyone mirrored Alice's excitement and dedication as they prepared for the network premiere.

As would remain the case for Welk's entire television career, critical reviews were mixed yet his audience grew every week, gaining an average of two rating points per week. Years later, Welk was to observe, "After twenty-seven years we finally struck it rich—and the press called us an 'overnight success.'"

"Some of the biggest critics reviewed the first show and said he'll [Welk] never last thirteen weeks."

—GEORGE CATES, musical director

Dodge was so pleased with "The Lawrence Welk Show" that they agreed to sponsor the series on a year-long basis. The announcement of that association led Welk to proclaim it as "one of the happiest moments of my life," and thus began an extraordinary kinship among Welk, Dodge, and the American public. It has been reported that forty-nine percent of the people who bought Dodges from 1952 to 1955 in southern California said they wanted to buy a Dodge because Lawrence Welk told them to buy one.

An extension of this unique and highly loyal bond between bandleader and audience was the emotional involvement viewers had with nearly every member of Lawrence Welk's Musical Family. People wanted to know the backgrounds and home lives of the performers whom they thought of as part of their own families. Each of them had been carefully chosen by Welk for their real, and not artificial, theatrical appeal.

As the years passed, Welk would eagerly search for new faces and exceptional talent to add to his television series. This was accomplished while on tour during each series hiatus, or on the band's annual three-week booking at Harrah's at Lake Tahoe, or during the television season when they appeared weekends at the Hollywood Palladium.

"Mr. Welk had a genius for choosing people that would fit in. He liked people who had a poor beginning or a struggle. He seemed to empathize with those people because he struggled for a long time. He liked dedication to working hard. He loved it if someone practiced. That was one thing Myron did."

—NORMA ZIMMER

Myron Floren shared with Welk an intense devotion to music from an early age, and their friendship undoubtedly solidified when they discovered they both came from similar impoverished backgrounds.

Born in Webster, South Dakota, Myron began playing the accordion at the age of seven on a mail-order instrument. It was then that he developed his pattern of extraordinarily long hours of practice and rehearsal that has not changed to this day.

As a child, Myron won local amateur contests in piano and accordion, and put himself through college by giving accordion lessons. He then joined radio station KSOO in Sioux

Myron Floren.
(Courtesy George Thow Collection)

Falls and in 1944 enlisted in a USO unit that sent him to Europe to entertain the troops. Upon his discharge from the service, Floren joined a hillbilly music group called the Buckeye Four. It was during an engagement in St. Louis, Missouri, in 1949 that he met Lawrence Welk. Myron recalls: "My wife Berdyne and I decided to go dancing to celebrate her birthday. We went to Casa Loma Ballroom where Lawrence Welk was appearing with his band. We had met casually when I worked for the radio station. Mr. Welk noticed me dancing near the stage and asked me to come up on stage and play the accordion. At intermission, he asked me to join his band."

Singer Jim Roberts began his association with Lawrence Welk around the same time as Alice Lon in 1954, joining the group just prior to their national television exposure. Roberts was so determined to become a Welk Musical Family member that he went to the Aragon Ballroom on the pier of Pacific Ocean Park in Santa Monica, California, and introduced himself to Welk, who hired him immediately. Jim wasted no time and began performing with the band that very night. Luckily for Jim Roberts, "The Lawrence Welk Show" soon went nationwide and he became a featured performer as well as one who remained with the show for the duration—a long way from the days he spent as a dishwasher, gas station attendant, and window washer while waiting for his big break.

Jim Roberts.
(Courtesy Don Keck)

"When we first started, Larry Hooper sang 'Wake the Town and Tell the People.' That was before tape, and we'd use a disc. The record kept skipping and he'd sing, 'Wake the town and tell the people, wake the . . . wake the . . . wake the . . .' It was like a comedy bit because he seemed to be right in sync. The poor man was on the floor."

—DICK DALE

One of the most beloved original members of the Musical Family was Larry "Hoopy" Hooper, who delighted audiences with his expert piano playing and baritone. Hooper joined the Welk band in 1948 when they appeared at the Roosevelt Hotel in New York. Before this, Hooper had spent several years as a pianist with the Frankie Masters Orchestra and before that with George Olson and his band. When Larry and Welk met, the Maestro asked him to sing but Hooper was so shy he initially refused.

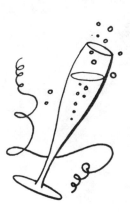

Larry Hooper.
(Courtesy Don Keck)

Hooper also has the distinction of recording a million-seller for Welk and Coral Records of "Oh Happy Day." The recording came about completely by accident one night at the Aragon Ballroom when Welk asked each band member to sing a number. Hooper's unrehearsed, spontaneous performance went over so well that he soon recorded the number, which became one of Welk's biggest hits.

All the performers, the band members, Sam Lutz, producers Don Fedderson and Ed Sobol, and, most of all, Welk himself, attempted to provide good music in a wholesome, attractive showcase fit for every member of their television family. ABC-TV provided the Welk show with set designer Charles "Chuck" Koon, who had the most unusual—and formidable—task of providing Lawrence Welk and His Champagne Music Makers with their now legendary trademark: the bubbles and the Champagne Bubble Machine.

Chuck Koon recalls: "Ed Sobol [the show's original producer] said we needed something to identify with champagne. I had been out with my kids to the Pomona Fair and saw the bubble machine. So I opened my mouth and Ed and Jim [Hobson] said it was a great idea. But the bubbles caused me nothing but twenty-seven years of problems! Bubbles are greasy. You had to protect the floor or somebody would slip. Through the years, we had them behind the orchestra, and had a bank of eight or nine fans to try to keep the bubbles blowing straight up. They'd get on the violin strings and the bow would slip. They'd spot the brass. They got on the heads of the drums. Cal Tech tried to make a bubble solution that wasn't greasy. They gave up."

As professional as "The Lawrence Welk Show" appeared, Welk and the entire group were learning as they went along in those early days of television. As Dick Dale said, "Nobody knew what was supposed to be done. I'd hardly even seen television let alone *done* it."

"The Lawrence Welk Show" had the distinction of being polished without being slick, professional without losing the essence of the warmth that made up the Lawrence Welk Musical Family. Welk believed in a tight rehearsal schedule leading up to a live broadcast, which itself was very efficiently produced, making it one of the most inexpensive yet lavishly mounted programs in the history of television.

"You had to work hard," remembers Dick Dale. "At one time, we were doing two TV shows ["Top Tunes and New Talent" and "The Lawrence Welk Show"] and working five nights a week down at the ballroom. If I had to do that now," he laughs, "I'd probably be dead!"

The schedule was a demanding one, both on the show's soundstage and off. Myron Floren explains, "We'd work till two o'clock in the morning at the ballroom, then report at eight o'clock in the morning so we would be ready for the television show. We would finish at seven o'clock, then we had two hours to stop by home for a bite to eat and then get to the ballroom and work till two o'clock the next morning. Even though we were tired to begin with we seemed to always get up for the show."

Certainly part of the enormous appeal of "The Lawrence Welk Show" was the sense of excitement always present in a live performance. And there was an unmistakable sense of family. As Dick Dale recalls, "It was a very close-knit group. [At that time] we only had about fifteen or seventeen people in it. We'd have parties together, and everything. At the end it wasn't at all [like that] because there were about fifty people. Sometimes you had to hurry to get on the bandstand to get a seat!"

One of the earlier traditions—and an example of how things could go wrong and turn out unpredictably right during the broadcast—was the cast members' spouses and children joining them on camera during the Christmas show. As Welk remembers, the first Christmas show was a disaster. He began the tradition by inviting the band to bring their children down to appear on the broadcast. Much grabbing of the spotlight resulted as doting parents made certain that the proud grandparents at home got a good close-up look at all of them. By air time, tempers flared and the babies were fidgeting and crying to such a degree that the show's timing was off. By the time Santa Claus appeared pulling his sleigh loaded with presents, time had run out. The program ended with the yelling and tears of indignant children demanding presents. Welk considered the whole show to be so terrible that he seriously thought about calling the sponsor and offering to resign. At Sunday Mass the following morning, however, the parishioners at St. Martin of Tours Church in Brentwood applauded Welk, remarking how much they enjoyed the Christmas show and adding that the same things happened at their houses. "It was just like home." Welk observed almost with surprise "how much the human touch counts."

A Welk Christmas tradition.
(Courtesy George Thow Collection)

The Lennon Sisters: (clockwise) Dianne (top),
Peggy, Janet, and Kathy. (Courtesy Kathy Lennon)

The most noticeable aspect of the first Christmas program of the series was the television network debut of four talented girls who would, perhaps more than any others, be synonymous with "The Lawrence Welk Show": the Lennon Sisters.

Kathy Lennon recalls that she and her sisters Dianne, Peggy, and Janet "started singing when we were little children. The first time the Lennon Sisters sang on stage was at our church musical. We did a little Scotch medley and at the end, we joined our Dad and his brothers in a number—there were eight of us—called 'Dry Bones.' We were the four little bones and they were the big bones."

The number went over so well that it led to a booking at the local Lions Club for twenty dollars. The girls' father told them of the offer, adding, "If you could do a few of these type of things, maybe we could add a dormitory on to the house." At the time, the Lennons shared a two-bedroom house. "There were eight children, our Mom and Dad, and Grandmother," explains Kathy. "We began doing a few service clubs around town for ten and twenty dollars." After performing at several of these functions, sister Dianne entered Santa Monica High School, where she met fellow student Larry Welk, Jr.

In October 1955 Larry Welk invited Dianne to a Halloween party at his home. She declined, explaining she had to sing at the Lions Club in Santa Monica that evening. He offered to pick her up there and bring her to the party and she accepted. Larry happened to arrive a little early and found "Dee Dee" performing in an act with her younger sisters. He had assumed, according to Kathy, that Dianne was "singing in a choral group or something," not aware that it was a family act. Larry was so taken with their talent that he immediately thought to tell his father of his "discovery." The sisters, however, assumed it was only talk and dismissed Larry's offer to arrange, in effect, an audition.

Kathy Lennon relates the following events: "About a month later, Larry called and said, 'My Dad's home sick with a cold and cannot get out of the house. Get over here quick and sing for him. I've been bugging him so much he just said, "Bring them over."' So we did. We went over to the house and Mr. Welk came out in his smoking jacket and velvet slippers. He said, 'My son has told me so much about you. You'd better be good.' He sat down on the couch and said, 'Sing for me.' So the four of us had a little pitch pipe and we hit the note and sang the spiritual 'He,' a cappella. He just sat there with his

Dianne, Janet, and Lawrence, 1956. (Courtesy Kathy Lennon)

mouth open and said, 'My, my, didn't my boy find something good!' He said, 'I'm going to call my musical director [George Cates] on the phone. Will you sing to him? He's just had a heart attack and will you sing over the phone?' So we sang over the phone. George said, 'Who have you got there, the McGuire Sisters or something?' He said, 'No. I've got a little neighborhood group that I think would be wonderful on our show.'

"Mr. Welk then said, 'I want to know how my audience is going to receive you. We are doing a Christmas show for the Sisters—the Daughters of Mary and Joseph Nuns who have a convent up on San Vincente in Santa Monica.' He said, 'Myron Floren's going to be there and I would love to have you girls come and sing. And if they like you, I want you to be on my Christmas show.' So we did."

Welk recalls that he was "amazed and enchanted. They were young and untrained but they had a freshness and a verve about them that I loved."

The unique sound of the Lennon Sisters that so captivated Welk and the American public was the result of the girls' mimicking the voices of their other family members. Kathy explains: "Peggy copied Uncle Teddy, who sang the high tenor. My Grandpa taught me the baritone. Dee Dee carried the lead. Janet was so little that she'd sing the lead sometimes and she also did a lot of solos. That was our sound—basically barber shop—a very intricate, four-part harmony."

The Lennon Sisters were such an immediate sensation that Welk asked the girls to join the show on a regular basis after only their second appearance. In short order, the Lennon Sisters became the "children" of the Welk television audience, generating incredible loyalty. Kathy Lennon explains, "It changed our lives in that we were viewed by the public in a different way. We were touched by millions and millions of Americans. We got fan mail by the thousands each week—bags and boxes of them. Every birthday we would get presents. Anything the fans knew we collected, they would send. Home-made gifts, home-made sweaters. Then as we got married, wedding gifts, and as we had children, baby gifts. We have been very fortunate that the American public has not been fickle. They have followed us from day one and we are now in our twenty-ninth year and we still have sell-out crowds wherever we go, I think because of the unique situation of being on "The Lawrence Welk Show." We were brought into their living rooms every Saturday night. We grew up at a time when Saturday night was Lawrence Welk, Sunday night was Ed Sullivan, and Tuesday night was Milton Berle."

"When we first started on the show, Janet had to wear white, almost clown makeup because she would blush so badly that she would turn dark. They couldn't figure it out the first few shows, why she was so dark and the other girls weren't. They ended up putting a little peanut light on her so it would brighten her clown makeup and it finally worked."

—KATHY LENNON

Welk and the Lennons' parents were in agreement that the girls' success should interfere as little as possible with having a "normal" childhood. "The director, Jim Hobson, was wonderful," recalls Kathy, "and our producer at the time, Ed Sobol, structured rehearsal time so that we could go to our regular schools. We would sing our songs and come home and make beds and change diapers. Nothing changed. It was the way to help a family with eleven children. We always thought it would end. The years just went on."

As much as the Lennon Sisters became a part of millions of American families, the behind-the-scenes crew on the show just as devotedly loved and protected the four sisters.

The Lennon Sisters, 1958. (Courtesy Kathy Lennon)

As head prop man on the show, Eddie Holland fondly remembers those days: "What a sweet bunch of children. It was game time all the time. We had squirt gun chases and things like that. It was a great family to be around."

Stage manager Ron Bacon recalls, "We put Janet on a box and watched the box get shorter and shorter as she got taller and taller. They lived a very sheltered, almost protected life. There was a kind of innocence that stayed with them and still does, I think. That innocent quality was part of their secret."

"The Lawrence Welk Show" grew even faster than the Lennon Sisters. Musical direc-

tor George Cates explains, "After the first year we added strings. At that time we had five brass, and we added a third trombone, then a fourth trumpet and a fourth trombone." Cates is credited by many for having been responsible for the expansion of the size of the band as well as its range of material.

Many of the musicians soon became viewer favorites and personalities in their own right early in the series. They included Barney Lidell (brass trombone), Norm Bailey (trumpet and double trombone), Bob Lido (solo singer and violinist), Buddy Merrill (guitar), Orie Amodeo (flute/sax/clarinet), Russ Klein (sax/clarinet/flute), Johnny Klein (drums), and Frank Scott (piano).

Ron Bacon, who later would become associate director, explains the unique "sweet" Champagne Music style: "Fundamentally, the Welk sound consisted of a strong rhythm section playing dance tempos and melodic lines that were very clear and easy to follow. Welk liked to hear the melody. He didn't like a whole lot of harmony. He would like unison parts. The secret to the show was at any time you would always know where the lead instrument was. That made the music accessible to the people."

Bacon appraises George Cates's contribution as that of "the person who stretched Lawrence's willingness to do things more than anybody else. George did have a way of creating some extra dimension on the show. He got it to be a little more sophisticated musically than it might have been. George was able to express to the band musically all the things that Lawrence wanted." Welk himself freely praises George Cates and calls him "a great talent. He's a genius! He's been a tremendous help not only to me but to the entire orchestra, and the band is much better today because of him." Cates observes, "The show was actually developed between the kicking back of ideas of a lot of professionals. I was in complete charge of the music. Jim Hobson was in complete charge of the picture and the production."

As the band improved, so did the show, as evidenced by the solid ratings it received each week. Yet a curious pattern emerged that would continue throughout Lawrence Welk's entire television career—neither he nor "The Lawrence Welk Show" would ever be nominated for an Emmy Award, the coveted honor bestowed by The Academy of Television Arts and Sciences for excellence in performance or technical achievement. Lawrence Welk's amazing popularity and loyalty from his audience seemed to be matched only by his conspicuous exclusion from any television industry awards bestowed by his peers.

Ron Bacon recalls, "The show set a standard for music shows at that time. I don't think there was ever a better organized, better planned show of that type. We were also known for the quality of our sound. I think we set a standard for the industry."

Despite that, no technical or performance Emmy award nominations were forthcoming at the close of their first season, leading TV critic Hal Humphrey to write in a 1955 article for the *Detroit Free Press:* "I don't know that all the critics and the TV Academy are all against Lawrence Welk. It is true that Lawrence failed to get an Emmy nomination last week, but some of his critics approach his TV programs much the same way they would Walt Disney's "Mickey Mouse Club." . . . Maybe the critics and other performers are tired of eulogizing those performers who attain their success by dint of only hard work or just being themselves. Welk has diligently applied himself since the days he helped around the farm in Strasburg, North Dakota. I doubt that even his most fervent fans would credit him with being the Heifetz of the Accordion, however. . . . His personality holds a sort of shy, clodhopper charm and heaven knows he is sincere. But perhaps in entertainment and critical circles there is a growing feeling that more aesthetic qualities should be required to qualify for genuine stardom. Arthur Godfrey, Ed Sullivan, and Tennessee Ernie Ford were blanked out by the Academy this time, too. Maybe for the same reason. It is possible we are returning to an age in show business when the performers will be referred to as artists."

"Top Tunes and New Talent" set, 1956.
(Courtesy Wally Stanard)

As *Look* magazine observed in 1957: "Nobody likes him but the public."

"The Lawrence Welk Show" was, in fact, so popular that what now would be called a "spin-off" program was created. "Lawrence Welk's Top Tunes and New Talent," sponsored by Plymouth, premiered on October 2, 1956, on ABC Monday evenings. The show featured Welk, the Lawrence Welk Orchestra, and promising new hopefuls in addition to the regulars from "The Lawrence Welk Show." (In 1958, the program was changed to "The Plymouth Show" and moved to Wednesdays until it went off the air in May 1959.)

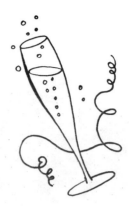

Joe Feeney. (Courtesy Don Keck)

Important to the Welk show was the discovery of "new talent": singer Maurice Pearson (on the show from 1957–60), Irish tenor Joe Feeney, and tap dancer Jack Imel; the latter two would become permanent fixtures on "The Lawrence Welk Show."

Joe Feeney joined "The Lawrence Welk Show" in January 1956, the first time he had ever traveled west from his home state of Nebraska. He had started singing as a boy soprano in the church choir in Grand Island, Nebraska, and continued his love of music through college studies, the army, and a subsequent solo spot in Arlene Francis's "Talent Patrol" television series. Joe's singing for a local radio program, "WOW Calling," led the station manager there to send tapes of Joe

Feeney's lyrical tenor voice to the Welk offices in California. Welk was so impressed that he offered Joe a job on his show, and Feeney promptly packed up his family, left his position as a salesman at a publishing firm, and joined Welk's Musical Family, where he remained for the next two decades.

Rhythm player and dancer Jack Imel made such a hit upon his first appearance on "Top Tunes and New Talent" in January 1957 that he was a regular on both that program and on "The Lawrence Welk Show." (Jack was in the navy and wore his uniform when he made his first Welk appearance.) Jack began tap dancing lessons at the age of four and later took up the xylophone, drums, the marimba, and vibes. While attending the Arthur Jordan Conservatory of Music in Indianapolis, Indiana, he tried out for the Horace Heidt troupe and impressed them with his showstopping routine of playing the marimba and dancing at the same time. In 1952, he enlisted in the navy and toured with Heidt for a navy recruiting campaign.

In 1955 Imel was an all-navy talent contest winner, which led to an appearance on "The Ed Sullivan Show." The next year found him again among the talent winners and back on the Sullivan show, which was followed by a cross-country tour of the United States. When Jack returned to his base in San Diego, he sent Lawrence Welk a recording of his marimba playing and landed the audition that led to his appearance on "Top Tunes and New Talent."

*Bobby Burgess, Jack Imel, and Art Duncan
performing the "challenge dance."*
(Courtesy Don Keck)

Between 1957 and 1959, hymn singer and legendary Dixieland clarinet player Pete Fountain was also a member of the cast of "The Lawrence Welk Show." In Fountain's case, his departure in 1959 was simply due to his feeling that he could not blend his Dixieland jazz playing into the sweet Champagne Music sound. It was an amicable parting, and Fountain went on to find his place as one of the jazz world's most respected musicians.

"A musician came up and said, 'Lawrence, I'm late for rehearsal and I have no excuse.' Lawrence looked at him and said, 'That's no excuse!'"

—**RALPH PORTNER**, announcer

In 1959, some important changes occurred for "The Lawrence Welk Show." After a very successful association with Dodge, the auto manufacturer chose to redirect its advertising dollar—and revise its image—by appealing to the so-called "youth market." While the "old guard" at Dodge regretted the decision, the choice was made. Welk remembers the break as a parting on "the most friendly terms" and quickly found another sponsor, the J. B. Williams Company—manufacturer of Geritol, Aqua Velva, Sominex, and Rose Milk. For more than twenty years, those products became as associated with Welk as Dodge had been, leading Welk to quip: "If you want to know how I keep my health and strength, I can only tell you that I play golf religiously, swim daily, think good thoughts, take Geritol in the morning, Sominex at night, and sprinkle on a little Aqua Velva in between!"

Geritol prevails over "The Lawrence Welk Show." (Courtesy Don Keck)

Honky-tonk ragtime piano player Jo Ann Castle. (Courtesy George Thow Collection)

Ragtime pianist and accordionist Jo Ann Castle made her first television appearance with Lawrence Welk in 1958 and returned for the New Year's Eve show that same year. In August 1959, Welk asked her to become a permanent member of the Musical Family and, significantly, Jo Ann Castle became the first woman to crack the all-male barriers of the Champagne Music Makers (cellist Charlotte Harris would join the band in 1961).

Jo Ann began piano lessons at a young age, but grew interested in the accordion when she attended a performance of Welk's when she was 10. She became so proficient in playing the instrument that at the age of 15 she became the accordionist and singer on Tex Williams's radio show.

Jo Ann debuted on television at age 17 on "The Ina Ray Hutton Show," which led to an appearance on Arthur Godfrey's "Talent Scouts" program and later his daytime show. Jo Ann then formed the Castle Quartet (Jo Ann and three men) and played engagements in Las Vegas before her initial appearance with Welk.

Jo Ann had a more difficult time than most in becoming accepted as part of Welk's Musical Family. Jo Ann sparked much viewer mail—some positive, but also a good many critical letters that complained about her method of playing the ragtime piano and about her personality. Some of the audience felt that Jo Ann's playing was sloppy—that she didn't hit the notes clearly and cleanly and sloughed off the difficult parts without real musicianship. The volume of mail convinced Welk that he should allow Jo Ann to read these comments. Welk brought a portion of the mail down to the Aragon one night and put it in Jo Ann's dressing room before he went on stage. Later, Welk found Jo Ann in her dressing room, crying and saying as she indicated the pile of letters, "How can people be so mean? How can they say such terrible things?" He told her frankly that some of the complaints were true and suggested that she practice at least an hour every day. Jo Ann agreed and began to practice sometimes up to four hours a day. Welk's advice, as always, was correct. Jo Ann's playing improved greatly and soon letters began to swing in her favor.

Another transition during Welk's 1959 season was the departure of Champagne Lady Alice Lon, which would become one of the show's most highly publicized—and controversial—events.

Alice Lon, by all accounts, was a warm, enthusiastic performer, liked by cast and crew alike. Prop man Eddie Holland remembers Alice as a "very lovely lady; very sincere, very kind and sweet, a very outgoing personality." Dick Dale remembers her as "a great gal, a great performer, a great voice, and funny, too."

Dick also appraises her stage demeanor: "She was the coolest. Nothing fazed her. We were doing a show in Texas, live, and she had about fifteen seconds before we started. We were doing a duet and she came out, putting on her gloves and asking, 'What's my first line?' She went through the song and didn't

goof a lyric." This so unnerved Dick that he recalls laughingly, "So *I* goofed the lyrics!"

Top makeup artist (and now head of that department at ABC) Rudy Horvatich served as Welk's own makeup man as well as for others on the series, including Alice Lon. He had a somewhat different opinion of her. "Alice was riding high all the time. She wasn't as disciplined as most of the musicians. The singers in a band have a little more freedom. Alice, of course, was well liked and made quite a name for herself, but she was nervous a lot of the time. She just wasn't feeling well, health-wise. She did have some kind of medical problem."

According to Dick Dale, Alice's "medical problem" was an unusual skin disease that affected her hands. "The skin would harden," remembers Dale, "the underlayer of the skin, not the outer. If she would hit herself on a table, her skin would crack and start to bleed."

Physical ailments aside, there are numerous and varied accounts explaining the Champagne Lady's exit from "The Lawrence Welk Show." Rudy Horvatich offers this explanation: "One notion is that she became too demanding. I think in her case, Lawrence gave her a wide berth, allowing her more privileges than he did the others."

Rudy also reveals, "There were times when she did things that would send Lawrence into an 'insane asylum.'" Rudy was present on one occasion "when Lawrence said, 'Alice, you're Alice from Dallas. Watch it or you might be Alice *in* Dallas!'" Which was a beautiful way of setting the law down."

Alice's discontent seems to have had more than one cause. Resident photographer Don Keck states: "Alice complained about the quality of the sound because she was out of breath from having to run back and forth to change costumes. I also recall that Lawrence criticized her outfits, saying her neckline was too low. He had the final word and said, 'No, I don't want this on the show, it's a family show.'"

Alice Lon duets with Dick Dale, 1958.
(Courtesy Don Keck)

Video control operator Wally Stanard has yet another explanation for Alice Lon's departure. "Alice sang a song and Lawrence didn't like the way she sang it. She insisted that she was going to sing it that way. That was the story and then Alice just left and went back to Texas."

Welk was of the belief that her agents had influenced her, arguing that Welk was hampering her solo career and that he did not spotlight her sufficiently. At the time, Welk was quoted as saying, "She quit for purely professional reasons, and I didn't even know she had quit till I read it in the papers."

Video control operator Wally Stanard (left) with producer-director Jim Hobson. (Courtesy Wally Stanard)

Whatever the reasons, when Alice Lon left the Champagne Music Makers were without a Champagne Lady. Luckily for all concerned, George Cates was instrumental in finding a replacement.

"I brought Norma Zimmer on the show," reveals Cates. "She worked for me at Coral Records. At the time Alice Lon left, we were auditioning girls and I brought Norma over and Welk flipped for her and we just put her on."

Norma admits: "It was a surprise to me when Mr. Welk called and asked me to come and do the little four-bar solo on the Thanksgiving show. It was just another job and I went there thinking, well, that should be an interesting day. His invitations to return were always a surprise to me."

Norma Zimmer had a highly successful career prior to joining "The Lawrence Welk Show" as a backup and choral singer. ("It's forty-three years in the business for me, and I've hardly been out of work for one week.") In her early days in California, Norma was a member of the Girl Friends Quartet, appeared regularly on several radio programs, and on television appeared on the original Dinah Shore series and Eddie Fisher's "Coke Time" program, among others. Norma also sang top soprano with the Norman Luboff Choir, the Voices of Walter Schumann, the Peter King Chorale, and the Ken Darby Singers. In addition, Norma was a favorite of Nelson Riddle and Gordon Jenkins and did background singing for such stars as Judy Garland, Frank Sinatra, Doris Day, Dean Martin, and Nat King Cole. By the time of her first Welk appearance, Norma had toured extensively with Carmen Dragon and had done "dozens" of Disney film soundtracks, television commercials, and feature films, including *Mr. Music* with Bing Crosby.

Although Norma had only a one-line solo she recalls that Welk was quite pleased with her work on his Thanksgiving-theme record album, commenting, "My, you have a pretty voice." "A few weeks later," explains Norma, "Mr. Welk called and said, 'Would you come and do that solo on the show?' I said I'd be happy to. And that day, Joe Feeney got laryngitis. So, Mr. Welk said, 'Do you have another song you could do? We have to fill Joe's spot.' I called Randy [her husband] and said, 'Get my "Smoke Gets In Your Eyes" arrangement down here right away.' We sight read it and did it live on the show. It was absolutely out of the blue, I never expected it."

The following week Welk called her again. "He said, 'Well, well, I had *many* phone calls after your appearance. Would you come back and do another show with us?' Naturally, I accepted with great delight."

Week after week, Norma Zimmer returned to "The Lawrence Welk Show" by popular demand, often in a duet with Jim Roberts. Norma was asked to appear on the New Year's Eve program of 1960 and "in front of the camera, Lawrence Welk invited me to become a member of his Musical Family. I felt the shock come into my face. The audience, seeing that look of amazement, asked later if it had been rehearsed because it seemed exaggerated. But it wasn't; it was entirely spontaneous. I accepted on the spot."

Norma tells of the meeting she and her husband, Randy, had with their two young sons, Mark and Ron: "We had a little family conference. We usually did that when we had big decisions to make. I asked the boys, 'I've been invited to do "The Lawrence Welk Show." Now, will that bother you? Will you feel embarrassed?' They said, 'Oh, no, Mom. Go ahead. None of our friends watch that show anyway.'"

"Mr. Welk is very generous with his talent and his time. He would come out and play for the people at our mobile home parks. I would never have dreamed of asking him but he always volunteered."

—NORMA ZIMMER

Norma Zimmer in her pre–Champagne Lady days, 1946. (Courtesy Norma Zimmer)

34

Lawrence Welk welcomes his new Champagne
Lady, Norma Zimmer, in 1961. (Courtesy Norma Zimmer)

In August 1961 Lawrence Welk officially gave the title of Champagne Lady to Norma Zimmer who, surprisingly, had mixed feelings about the label. "Well, it bothered me when he first invited me to be Champagne Lady. I thought, oh dear, beer lady, whiskey lady. It just did something to me. But then he kept saying, 'Norma, my music is champagne music. It only means effervescent personality, bubbly personality, bubbling music.' Which is true. I finally said yes and I haven't regretted it. It's a lovely title. I enjoyed it and it has made a great difference in my life and my career."

Of Norma Zimmer, Welk has said, "Norma just radiates the kind of spiritual serenity which comes from true religious faith, and she is such a fine artist I still wonder how I could ever have been so fortunate to have her with us."

From the time Norma Zimmer made her first appearance on "The Lawrence Welk Show" at Thanksgiving 1959 to her crowning as Champagne Lady in August 1961, there had been two major additions to the Lawrence Welk Musical Family: the dancing team of Bobby Burgess and Barbara Boylan and the second woman after Jo Ann Castle to join the Champagne Music Makers—cellist Charlotte Harris. (Strictly speaking, though, Jo Ann Castle may be considered a specialty act and solo artist rather than an orchestra member, making Charlotte Harris the first woman to be a bona fide member of the band.)

Charlotte recalls, "My mother was a very fine violinist and later on she had a music school, which turned out to be the biggest music school on the west side of Chicago. She started me on the piano when I was three and the cello when I was four and a half. The cello was mainly so I could be in the orchestra with my older sister but, of course, as I grew up over the years I played both instruments professionally. I was strictly a classical musician until I moved to California. That was in 1952." By the time she graduated from Northwestern University in

Evanston, Illinois, with a bachelor of music degree, Charlotte's parents had relocated to California. Charlotte became so enamored with its warm climate during a brief visit there that she decided to stay and make it her home.

"I was working in the movie studios out here when Mr. Welk had a cellist in his band by the name of Dave Pratt. David decided that he was going to leave the show and asked me if I was interested in the job and I said no. I was still working in the movie studios and doing classical work. I had never watched "The Lawrence Welk Show," but I began tuning it in on Saturdays and discovered that they were trying a different cello player each week. Well, Dave talked to George Cates about me and they asked me to play. I went over and auditioned at the Aragon and then I played a solo on the television show.

"That was in March of 1961. There's a union rule that if you play three weeks in succession they have to hire you for a thirteen-week cycle. Well, they had someone else, evidently, they wanted to try. So that third week I would have played, they tried someone else, but after the show was over, they called me up and gave me the job."

When asked if it was more difficult being a female Champagne Music Maker, Charlotte replied: "I really didn't feel that I was special. I got loads of fan mail from women who thought it was wonderful, and from men, too. Lawrence liked that. Whatever the fans liked, I think is what Lawrence liked."

Charlotte concludes: "I always knew that being a woman and being able to get a job like that you had to be at least as good as the fellows—or better. All I ever got were compliments. We all felt like family."

So, as in the cases of Norma Zimmer, Jo Ann Castle, and the Lennon Sisters, the invitation to become part of the Lawrence Welk Musical Family was a combination of Welk's unerring eye for talent, personality, and professionalism and, just as important, positive

Charlotte and her cello. (Courtesy Don Keck)

viewer reaction. Seldom, if ever, has any celebrity or television host given so much consideration to his audience's opinions. Such feedback could quite literally decide whether a performer would remain on the program or be released, and in a few cases such as Jo Ann Castle's, audience response could provide insight into how a performer might increase his or her appeal.

Welk inaugurated a system called the "fever chart," which listed the name of all the performers, the ratio of positive and negative mail, and the type of music most requested and most disliked, and so forth. "One of the main reasons for our success has been the devotion and support of our fans, and they are a tremendously important part of our daily business life. What they think and what they want is of vital importance to us," Welk has stated.

The young, attractive dance team of Bobby Burgess and Barbara Boylan also became a regular on the series as a result of an avalanche of fan mail following the team's appearances, requesting more of the vivacious teenagers' dance routines.

Despite his young age, Bobby Burgess was a show business veteran of sorts, having begun dance lessons at the age of three which had led to appearances on more than sixty television programs, including being a Mouseketeer on "The Mickey Mouse Club" for three years. Bobby met Barbara Boylan when they were both twelve years old. "I won a scholarship to the dance school she was going to," says Bobby. "Bobby and I were unique," notes Barbara, "because we were best friends. We were like brother and sister."

Bobby and Barbara's friendship—and later their audition for the show—came about because Barbara's parents, she says, "were very much Welk fans. They listened to all of his music." In the spring of 1961, Bobby and Barbara hoofed it down to the Aragon Ballroom in Santa Monica, where Welk still appeared regularly.

"Welk saw us in the audience and he couldn't believe that young kids could dance ballroom, so he got us up on stage, and boy,

From beginning to end: Bobby and Barbara dance through a winter wonderland in one of their last routines together.
(Courtesy George Thow Collection)

Barbara and Bobby. (Courtesy Barbara Boylan)

we were dancing all kinds of dances! He came out with the idea of a 'Calcutta' contest—that was his big hit—and Bobby and I won," explains Barbara.

Bobby then went on tour with Marie Wilson and returned at the time Welk was playing the Hollywood Palladium ballroom. Again, Bobby and Barbara planned their "appearance."

As Bobby remembers, "We were standing in the front row with our red outfits on and Mr. Welk said, 'Oh, the "Calcutta" dance contest winners are down there. Would you like to come up and do "Calcutta"? We said, 'No, we'll do "Yellow Bird." Then he asked us on the TV show the next week. He always said that we created a job for ourselves. Every week we did something else. Six months later on the air, he announced that we were regulars. I always remember Lawrence referring back to 'The Mickey Mouse Club' and saying to me, 'You've never given me any trouble, because you were raised by Walt Disney.' What more family-type shows could I have been on than 'The Walt Disney Show' and 'The Lawrence Welk Show'?"

Barbara also recalls the unusual manner in which they learned they were "permanent": "We read in the paper that we had signed a contract. We really hadn't signed a contract, our agreement was verbal."

Barbara believes that one of the reasons why they so delighted Lawrence was that, "We created all our own dances and went out and did research with other choreographers." Bobby adds, "I always loved it because I got to do my own choreography and Lawrence left me alone. Although he was a good ballroom dancer himself, Lawrence never interfered because he knew we put in hours and hours on the side, rehearsing in front of a mirror."

Joining the show early on, and at the age of nineteen, now gives Barbara Boylan another perspective: "We were creating a job. The partners that took my place [Cissy King and Elaine Niverson] started right at the top. Bobby and I worked ourselves up the ladder.

> "The show to me, besides being fun and a good job, was also a means to build a name so I could go on the outside and make more money. I usually figured that the income from the Welk show and from the company represented about 20 percent of what I made."
>
> —MYRON FLOREN

It didn't feel like real stardom, we were just working. We did it for sheer fun and the money was like a bonus. We were paying for our own choreography. We didn't make anything, but it was sure fun. Then, through the years it grew, our popularity grew and by the time I left [1967], we had lots of opportunities."

Bobby explains, "Lawrence always said, 'I pay scale on my show, but if you get popular, you can make good money on the outside.' He was right. Better dates started coming in for us and I still work through Welk's personal manager, Sam Lutz."

Barbara and Bobby view Lawrence as the "ideal employer," although they clearly see him as more than that. As Barbara says, "I love Mr. Welk. He was super to me. We were really hard workers, and he appreciated that and was very good to us. He'd say, 'What could I do to help you?' We needed a record player so he bought us a record player, one that I still use today. And he would let us use his Palm Springs home. He was a father figure."

On Lawrence Welk, Bobby states, "He gave me artistic freedom. He knew we were putting in all those extra hours in his behalf, and he liked people who worked hard.

"There were about four things he always conveyed to me: Be prepared; don't be fat, stay thin; don't be late; and no drinking on the job. Those were his four basic unwritten laws. He has great discipline."

"We did it for sheer fun" —*Barbara Boylan.*
(Courtesy Don Keck)

The only difficulty that Barbara recalls of those early years was a conservative policy regarding her wardrobe. "I couldn't show my legs at first," she reveals. "That was difficult. I had to wear pettipants so the tops of my legs wouldn't show. Our first producer [Ed Sobol] was kind of old-fashioned. As times went on, things got easier."

Welk quickly instilled in the young dance team the importance of the audience. As Barbara observes: "He would always sign autographs, and we always did, too. Because that was important. Nobody would just run away after a show. Maybe you'd want to and you were dripping wet but it was important that we all respect our fans."

Jazz babies Barbara Boylan, Lawrence Welk, and Norma Zimmer. (Courtesy Norma Zimmer)

Norma Zimmer believes one of the reasons Lawrence Welk has never lost his popularity and why his audience is uncommonly loyal is that "he listened to what his audience liked. He had secretaries answering his mail and every letter that had suggestions or comments was listed. When requests came in, they listed how many times a song was requested. He gave the people what they wanted to hear. I think that's the reason for his success. He loved his audience, it was genuine. He always wanted to please. Mr. Welk sent out love over that show, and I always tried to send out love. I think everyone who appeared on that show was loved by the audience." Norma now extends that devotion to fans in her own personal appearances. "In all my concerts, I stay until the last person leaves, to sign autographs and chitchat or give someone a hug because I do love the audience."

Welk's deep reverence for his public seems to have existed not only from the earliest days of his television career, but long before—in fact, from the days of his cross-country ballroom engagements.

Announcer Ralph Portner explains Welk's realization of the importance of the public from his days on the road: "Lawrence learned a long time ago about building a fan club. He would send you a postcard, once you had written and you were on his list. He'd say, 'Dear so-and-so, I'm going to be in your hometown.' Everybody who got a card would think, 'Hey, he's acknowledged me.' An hour or so before a show, if the capacity were six hundred, there would be maybe eight hundred people waiting in line. He catered to the people. He mingled with the people.

"He loved his fans and would do anything for them" —Rudy Horvatich. (Courtesy George Thow Collection)

People like to be acknowledged and recognized. Say, for instance, you would come to the show with your wife. Lawrence would come down and say, 'May I dance with your lovely wife?' Naturally your wife is going to be flattered. He'd start dancing and say, 'Oh my, I don't have anyone to lead the band. Would you be kind enough to conduct the orchestra?' Afterwards, the wife would say, 'I danced with Lawrence Welk and you should have seen my husband leading the band!'"

Myron Floren observes, "Lawrence was very organized and dedicated. I could sense in him a quality of persistence that I have seen in few other men. He would dictate letters while we were riding, and when we arrived at our destinations his secretary, Lois, would type them up and mail them. As we prepared to enter a new town, Lawrence would check a list of any old friends he might have in the area so that names and families would be fresh in his memory when he greeted them."

Welk's makeup man, Rudy Horvatich, states, "I don't think I've known any other entertainer who has given so much of his time back to the fans. He seemed to owe some allegiance to the fans that very few people understand. He loved his fans and would do anything for them."

Horvatich also reveals that Welk was indeed humble about his success and was far removed from the well-publicized scandals of Hollywood. "For the first few years, I think he was astonished at the things that were happening. He didn't believe he was creating such a sensation. And he was. He never indicated he was aware that he was important and a very big man in the entertainment business." Rudy adds, "He was *nervous* about it. But, as time went on, and each year ABC signed a year's contract—which few of them did in those days—then I guess he knew he was creating a sensation in this country."

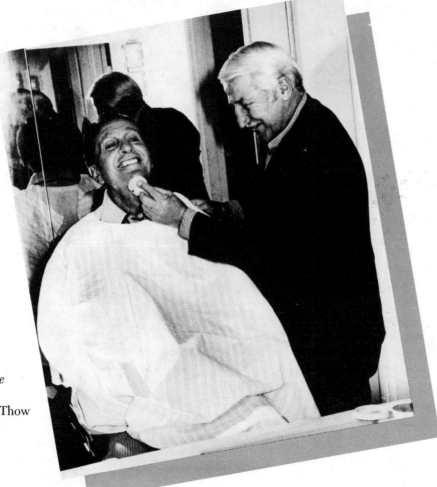

Rudy Horvatich prepares Lawrence for his program.
(Courtesy George Thow Collection)

One of the important elements of Welk's lasting success was his instinctive sense of hiring the very best people to work with him, all finely tuned to understanding him and presenting a program that was truly an "entire production supervised by Lawrence Welk." As musical arranger Joe Rizzo observes, "Lawrence had the last word. In fact, he'd change the show after the dress rehearsal if he didn't like the way a number came off. He'd just take it out or substitute it. He was honest in the way that he wanted to do his music. He wouldn't let anybody tell him that he was wrong. After all, he was the boss."

Video control operator Wally Stanard confirms Welk's very definite idea of what his audience wanted—and there was no better judge of his audience's taste than Welk himself. "All the music on the show was approved by Lawrence. If he listened to rehearsal—he was in his dressing room and he had a special speaker set up—and if he didn't like one number he'd say so. *Everything* was with his approval," states Stanard.

Aside from George Cates (who perhaps understands Welk musically more than anyone else), one other man was to become the primary force in carrying out Welk's ideas and philosophy of entertainment, combining artistry and Welk's Champagne Music. Director Jim Hobson became the show's producer as well after the original producer, Ed Sobol, passed away. Hobson quickly gained the respect of cast and crew alike, all having uniformly high praise for him. Welk has said that Jim Hobson was solely responsible for getting the show on the air and for keeping it mov-

ing. Welk considers him "the finest director for a musical show in television."

Veteran cameraman Mike Freedman, who himself has gained considerable notoriety ("I have eight Emmys and yet I am remembered for two things—for being the cameraman who was hit by Woody Hayes on the air and for pioneering the use of the hand-held camera"), praises Jim Hobson's own innovations on "The Lawrence Welk Show." "It was Jim Hobson [who] was the glue that held the show together. Week in and week out he'd come up with creative things to do. He had a boundless supply of creative ideas. We used to call him 'St. James' because he never raised his voice. It was always his mistake and he always gave you the right to make a mistake. I guess that was Jimmy's philosophy. In so doing, you tried to do better than you knew you could. He brought creativity and tolerance and loving, kindness and gentleness."

Original producer Ed Sobol with Lawrence, 1960. (Courtesy Don Keck)

Lawrence's 1962 birthday celebration. (Courtesy
Don Keck)

*Jim Hobson and Lawrence confer during a commercial
break.* (Courtesy Don Keck)

Indicative of the close, symbiotic relationship between Hobson and Welk is a statement Hobson once made that echoes Mike Freedman's assessment of Hobson being "the glue that held the show together." Hobson said, "Lawrence maintains the idea that he is trying to train all of us to take over if or when he is out of the picture. But my argument to him has always been: 'Lawrence, the production staff is perfectly capable of putting on a good musical variety show, but without you the magic is gone.' You know when you think about it, Lawrence is what holds the whole show together."

The crew of "The Lawrence Welk Show"—cameramen, lighting directors, videotape operators, prop men, stagehands, cue card holders, and so on—was as much a part of the Lawrence Welk Musical Family as every performer and band member who appeared on camera.

Stage manager Ron Bacon remembers fondly, "It was a badge of honor to be part of that crew. Many of our best cameramen have been trained on that show. The program had such a good look to it and the quality was so high, we were used constantly as a reference throughout the industry."

Bacon also views his years on "The Lawrence Welk Show" as ones that gave him lasting friendships—and more than a few laughs. Bacon recalls, "When the director Jim Hobson was sick one time, he asked me to direct the show for him, which I did. After I finished the show there was a big box in the control room that was from Jim. I didn't know what it was but I stuck it in the back of my car and took it home. I opened it up and there was a live turkey. I left the room for a minute and when I came back, there was the turkey out of the box on the carpeted floor in front of the TV with my kids. Any plans of disposing of the turkey ended right there!"

Associate director Ron Bacon (center) with Lawrence and George Cates. (Courtesy Nick Pantelakis)

Head prop man Eddie Holland believes the closness of the cast and crew contributed to the show's popularity.

'I used to look forward to going to work, because of the friendships and camaraderie and the laughs and the fun. The whole crew was like one, big happy family."

There were many happy moments on- and off-camera and, as Eddie Holland recalls, funny incidents as well. The Maestro is legendary for his sense of humor in the form of "Welkisms"—spontaneous, inadvertently hilarious fractures of the English language. Holland recalls one such incident in which he was involved: "I was out in the truck when these cases came in. They had big letters on the side: 'FRAGILE.' So I put them on this two-wheel truck and wheeled them into Welk's office. Lawrence was there with his secretary [Lois Lamont] and Barney Liddell and a couple of other musicians. When I wheeled them in there I just said, 'Where do you want to put these?' Welk said, 'What are they?' Just jokingly, I looked at him and said, 'Well, it's ten cases of 'Fragilly.' He just looked at me and he looked at the cases and he turned to his secretary and said, 'Lois, did we order any of this "Fragilly?"' Lois didn't know what to say. I said 'Well, I don't know but here it is.' He said to open the boxes to see what was inside. So I opened one up and it was full of his albums. I pulled one out and said, 'Hey, they're albums.' He said, 'Oh, yes. Those are the albums we ordered. They probably put them in the wrong box!' He did a lot of things like that. But how are you going to argue with success?"

Lawrence and his secretary since 1945, Lois Lamont. (Courtesy Don Keck)

Associate director Jim Balden (who began on the show as a cameraman along with Herm Falk and Jimmy Angel) says he was "very flattered" to be hired, explaining, "It really was prestigious. It was the biggest thing that ABC had and it was keeping ABC out of the red."

Lawrence with cameraman Jim Balden.
(Courtesy Jim Balden)

Kathy Lennon fondly recalls, "We were so in love with all the crew members and all the band members. Everybody treated us like gold. I don't think there is another show on today that has children that they take care of so beautifully. On a big show like that where there were forty musicians and a crew of probably the same, they all sheltered us. There was not a 'damn' or a 'hell' said. And it was always, 'Excuse me, girls!' We had a ball with them. At that time, ABC was very young. It had two studios which were huge sound stages. [They] were originally the Norma Talmadge Studios on Prospect and Talmadge in Hollywood. The lot behind the building was just dirt. We would pull two light stands out and put up a volleyball net at lunchtime and play volleyball with the crew and the cameramen and all. Or we'd get the musicians to jam and we'd all dance. That's how we all learned to jitterbug."

As many crew members and musicians became close friends over the years, so did many of the performers. Norma Zimmer explained, "The girls on the show shared a dressing room and that is where friendships begin and grow," adding, "it really was like a family reunion each week." Norma, the Lennon Sisters, Jo Ann Castle, and Barbara Boylan became particularly close in those early days, and, as Norma states, "Now that we're apart, we girls still correspond."

Six other talented people were also indispensable—and dear friends—to the other members of the Musical Family: hairstylist Roselle Friedland; costumer Rose Weiss; set designer Charles "Chuck" Koon (the man responsible for giving bubbles to the Champagne Music Makers); George "Gus" Thow, who wrote the words Lawrence Welk spoke to his television audience; ace photographer Don Keck; and veteran makeup artist Rudy Horvatich.

"The Lawrence Welk Show" counts down to go on the air. (Courtesy Don Keck)

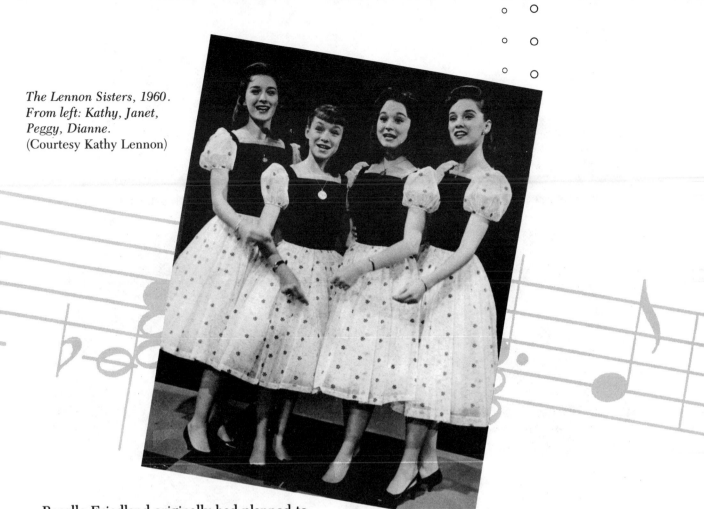

*The Lennon Sisters, 1960.
From left: Kathy, Janet,
Peggy, Dianne.
(Courtesy Kathy Lennon)*

Roselle Friedland originally had planned to help out her friend Rudy Horvatich for one show, but the job lasted as long as "The Lawrence Welk Show" was on television. "Rudy came to me and asked if I would do him a favor of working on Saturday [the day of the live broadcast] at the studio. After the show, all the kids said, 'Roselle, please stay with us.' That's how I got my job. They were really nice to work for. The Lennons, Barbara Boylan, Norma, and Jo Ann Castle—they were not spoiled. This was family. I went to all the weddings and baby showers."

As the cast grew—and particularly as the Lennon girls matured into beautiful women who married and had children—organizing baby showers was far less challenging than Rose Weiss's formidable task of creatively disguising their "delicate condition" with highly original costuming. Chuck Koon had the equally challenging job of designing sets that offered even greater camouflage.

Don Keck remembers, "When the Lennons were having their children, it was a run-ning thing with the wardrobe department, set decorator, and art director to design scenery and costumes that would camouflage the girls until the time the babies arrived, hiding them behind railings and furniture because they were pregnant."

"The pregnancies on that show were unbelievable!" declares Rose Weiss. "When we first started having them, Lawrence didn't want the audience to see pregnant women on the show. He was from the old school that when a woman is pregnant she doesn't go out in public. We were disguising them in all manners. We were hiding them behind an upright piano, or with Jo Ann Castle—we made her a chicken and had her in a half of an egg. With the Lennons, we did all sorts of things to disguise their condition. When you've got one person you can do something, but when you've got two or three doing a number together and only one is pregnant we had a tough time building sets around them."

For Lawrence, no knees is good knees.
(Courtesy Don Keck)

Of her still-unbroken association with Lawrence Welk and her position as costumer, Rose Weiss says, "No job is easy when you've got a big job to do. It was a difficult job in that you had to please everybody in what they were wearing. And that, of course, meant pleasing Lawrence Welk himself—and his audience. Lawrence used to get into costumes and I got him into the little short lederhosen pants one year and he got a letter from one woman who complained that she didn't like to see his bare knees. From that point on, Lawrence would never get into costume. Lawrence always liked to be dressed and he would never sit down in a costume or eat while he was wearing those clothes."

Chuck Koon worked side by side with Rose Weiss, as did director Jim Hobson, to give the show its distinctive, polished look. "Rose pretty much knew after a while what colors I liked to use and I knew what she liked. But if I thought there were going to be a problem, I'd call her up and say, 'Look, Rosie, this set is going to be all in bright red . . . keep the costumes light or they'll disappear into the background.'"

Recalling Ed Sobol, the show's first producer, Koon says, "Ed was great, he had a lot of great ideas. I'd swear he had insomnia, always calling me at home in the middle of the night, saying something like 'I think we'll do the Lennons' number in the schoolroom!'"

"Janet was doing, 'Lovely Lady Dressed in Blue, Teach Me How to Pray.' Just then, the monitor on stage cut off. There was no sound coming on the stage and it was going over the air. Janet didn't know what happened. All she knew was that the camera was still on. She continued to lip sync with no sound on the stage. Finally, the sound came back on. She never missed a beat."

—KATHY LENNON

Chuck Koon's relationship with Sobol's successor, Jim Hobson, was equally as inspired, a friendship begun years before they teamed for "The Lawrence Welk Show." "Jim Hobson and I went to school together. That's how long we've known each other. Jim would have an idea for a song or a number and he'd call me or we'd have a quick meeting. I always knew where we stood with the budget. There were things I could reuse or if Jim felt wealthy that week we would build a big set and reuse it at a later date. We'd have a cost-heavy show, then a light one to balance the budget."

Koon devised a complete cross-referenced filing system that would prove indispensable as the years passed. "I had pictures, I kept all the drawings. I've got file cabinets full of drawings back to the early shows—in those days we had special shows for all the holidays," explains Koon.

Koon estimates there were as many as eight complete sets per show, with the average being four. "Occasionally, they would opt for one big set," says Koon. "We did Venice and built a real canal! We used a lot of drapery and the crystal chandeliers. They all belonged to Teleklew [Welk's production company]. When the show finally finished, those things were given to San Diego State College. We hauled two or three big semis full of scenery down there. They'll be using the stuff for years."

Yet as opulent as the sets and the production values were, the show was legendary for being one of the most efficiently produced and inexpensive programs on television. Chuck Koon says he was never aware of any specific budget considerations or figures. "In twenty or thirty years, I never knew the budget from week to week, because Jim would not work on a week's budget at a time. He might work on a month's. I knew that if we were spending a lot of money on one week's show, the next week we would have to take it easy."

Champagne sets by Chuck Koon.
(Courtesy Don Keck)

Resident photographer Don Keck wa
fact hired initially to provide Koon with a
permanent photographic file of every set created for "The Lawrence Welk Show." Keck
had replaced Koon as technical director at
the Pasadena Playhouse when Koon joined
the program. Keck explains why photos of
the sets were so necessary: "They repeated
numbers. They'd get audience and fan mail
asking them to repeat numbers so they kept
all the pictures on file—Welk owned all the

sets and they were stored in the back room.
When they repeated the numbers, the art director would take these pictures to the production meeting and say, 'Well, this is what
we did at that time and we'll take this compo-
nent out of this set or we'll repeat this set
entirely, maybe change the color.'

"Then Rose Weiss decided she needed pictures of the wardrobe because they repeated
stuff and they wanted records of it. Then I
started shooting wardrobe pictures. Then the

talent started requesting talent pictures—and from that point on I shot for everybody.

"For one show, I was required to shoot still pictures, wide shots of the sets for the art director and the producer, and closer shots of the wardrobe for the wardrobe department. They were all dated and kept in a file so they could go back and refer to them."

Gus Thow had been a renowned Dixieland trumpet player and was hired by Welk on the spot after an impromptu audition at the Aragon Ballroom in April 1956. Of those early days he says, "When I first joined the band I thought it was pretty rinky-dink and 'Mickey Mouse,' but I was willing to go along with it and it did evolve. The band improved immeasurably over a period of years. It got to the point where it was one of the best bands in the country."

Thow remembers Welk with deep regard. "I'm eternally grateful for all that he did for me. He took me on at a time when a trumpet

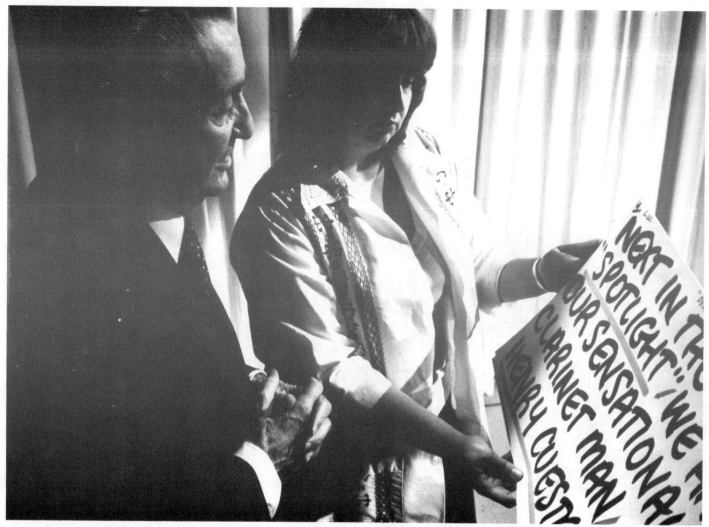

A crew member prepares Lawrence's cue cards during a broadcast. (Courtesy Wally Stanard)

player of my caliber, my style, was practically unwanted." After being with the show for several years and in his mid-fifties, Thow admits, "I realized my lip was gone." Welk then suggested Thow might make a full-time job out of writing and working on the production side of the show. This transition came about after Thow wrote some continuity bits and announcements for Welk that pleased Lawrence and Jim Hobson.

Of that task, Thow says, "I tried to write what was natural for him. A lot of people thought he got carried away with language. Lawrence talks to people in his own language. I'd be certain to write the sort of copy that Lawrence was comfortable with. When I became a full-time writer for the show we had a regular routine and I'd go out to him the day before taping and go over all the continuity. He would make the changes and I'd

56

George Thow reviews Welk's cue cards with him while on location in Escondido, 1976. (Courtesy Nick Pantelakis)

have the cue cards ready for him the next morning. I had often wished he would let me put just three or four words on a card and let him do things his own way. He got so locked into things that it [his delivery] got stiff. But he would not go on television without those cards. But when he'd get away from them and start ad-libbing a bit with a guest, he came off great. But for the most part, he was limited by those cards."

Dick Connolly, who was responsible for Welk's cue cards for the live broadcast of the show, remembers those days as "thrilling ones. The show was so popular that tickets were booked a year ahead.

"The excitement would start rolling after the dress rehearsal and as everything was falling into place the main concern of everybody was how Welk came across on camera. If he was comfortable with the cue cards, they knew the show would be okay. He had to have complete faith in whomever held the cue cards. You had to be exactly at the right spot. If you weren't, you were gone the next week. During the Christmas show of '63 someone else took over when I went on vacation. Welk was promoting his tour and he had to read five minutes of cards. The lettering on the cards was awfully big, so you might wind up with fifty or sixty cards. In pulling them, you had to be with his speech pattern and you couldn't miss a beat. You were performing along with him. Most peo-

ple can ad-lib if a card slips, so you aren't under the pressure, but with Welk you were. I was at home on my vacation watching the show and the kid dropped the cards on the floor. You saw Welk's head look down to the floor. You knew they were just grabbing cards and holding them up and they were getting so confused. He did not stop, he read whatever you put in front of him."

"Welk would introduce the songs from the cue cards. We were doing a medley from World War I. When they put the word 'one,' they made a Roman numeral. And when they were on the air live, he introduced the medley, 'And now we have a medley from World War Eye!'"

—EDDIE HOLLAND, head prop man

Although Connolly's association with Welk ended when Connolly was promoted to ABC's engineering department in 1964, he remains a firm supporter of Welk. "He was genuine with the audience. He was quite shy, actually. I don't think he was phony with anybody. Nothing was put on, what you saw up there was genuine. He never lost his humility." When Connolly left the show, "A lot of joy was gone. I felt like a performer, like I had participated in the show as much as Welk!"

Camera operator Mike Freedman offers, "There was a real sense of conviviality among the performers. Among the people who did the work I did—cameramen and crew—we really enjoyed each other."

Bob Ralston was an exceptionally talented master of the keyboard, beginning his career at the age of ten playing for dance studios for seventy-five cents an hour. When he was twenty-one, Bob landed a job playing piano with the Freddy Martin Orchestra of the famed Cocoanut Grove in Hollywood, where he remained for three years until September 1962. "During those years I started doing recording sessions," Ralston explains, "with Billy Vaughn and Ray Conniff and Lawrence Welk. In '62 at one of the Welk sessions, Lawrence was present at the studio and he liked what I was doing—some big arpeggio—and he invited me back. Then he invited me back in January of '63 and every week thereafter. I think about a month after, he announced to me and to the country that I was going to be a regular on the show."

The crew provides atmosphere moments before the cameras roll. (Courtesy Don Keck)

Bob Ralston. (Courtesy Don Keck)

Originally hired as a pianist and arranger, Ralston recalls in his first days how he acclimated himself to Welk's unreproachable sense of pleasing his audience: "I remember going to Lawrence in 1963 and saying, 'I've got a great idea for the four pianos. Let's do a series of Viennese waltzes.' He put his hand on my shoulder and said, 'Bob I've got to have a little talk with you. If we do Viennese waltzes, people are going to think we have an old-fashioned show. We have to do something modern and up-to-date like 'Nola' and 'The Doll Dance'!"

When Jerry Burke, who was resident organist, passed away Ralston offered to take his place. "Welk said, 'Bob, I don't understand why everybody wants to do something different. The dancers want to be singers, and the musicians want to be dancers.' I went back to him the next week and said, 'Lawrence, I know you said not to bring up the subject again, that you were going to hire somebody else to play the organ, but I wonder if you would consider for a moment how much money you would save if you didn't have to hire somebody else.' He said, 'Now that you mention it, maybe we'll give you a try!'"

*Norma Zimmer steps in for Dianne Lennon in
1964 when the eldest Lennon left the show to get
married.* (Courtesy Norma Zimmer)

Welk and young fan.
(Courtesy George Thow Collection)

By the mid-1960s, Lawrence Welk's popularity continued to grow at least as quickly as did his television cast. Critics, though, were sharply divided on Welk's musical talent, his demeanor, and his off-camera role as head of an expanding empire, which now included Teleklew Productions (Welk spelled backwards), a record company, numerous real estate holdings, and the acquisition of many music publishing companies. What could not be disputed by any critic, no matter how vitriolic his opinions, was Welk's incredible popularity. Hank Grant wrote in the *Miami Herald* in 1962: "Welk probably has the most loyal fan following of any personality on television. The demand for tickets to his show is so great that rarely can requests be filled less than six months in advance. That the younger ones are coming around is evidenced by the increased numbers of teenagers who appear at his record-breaking performances around the country. And that teenagers are buying his records is evidenced by the fact that his recording of 'Calcutta' is still selling, with a current total of 1,850,000 sales."

As a result of the controversies surrounding Lawrence Welk, his respect for hard work and discipline were often misinterpreted as unyielding, unreasonable, and tyrannical behavior. Yet there are remarkable numbers of people who have remained with him for an extraordinary number of years and are devoted to Welk and his strict work ethic. The number of musicians and performers who have left "The Lawrence Welk Show" is relatively small in relation to the duration and scope of the Welk organization.

Welk himself is quite candid in regard to his business and moral practices: "Self-discipline gives you a handle to keep your life under control and achieve far more joy and happiness than you could otherwise." And he does not spare himself, admitting: "I would much prefer to keep bounding out of bed at five every morning and spend the day working than take off on the most luxurious vacation in the world. A vacation doesn't interest me. I'd rather work."

Welk has been criticized for two other operating procedures: hiring performers with-

Peggy Lennon, Dick Dale, Aladdin, Joe Feeney, Kathy Lennon, and Norma Zimmer in a 1964 production number. (Courtesy Norma Zimmer)

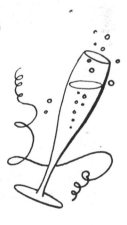

out written contracts and paying scale (minimum wages established by the American Federation of Television and Recording Artists [AFTRA], the show business union). On the issue of contracts, Welk feels there is no pressure in his system. He feels he encourages his people and opens up opportunities, but he never ties them down legally. "I wouldn't tie anyone up with a contract," he explains, "because to me, freedom is too precious. I think we work best in freedom; we develop our talents best." His policy is clear to his Musical Family—if they do the best they can they have a job for life.

Dick Dale affirms, "In 32 years, I never signed anything." Resident photographer Don Keck details, "Everybody on the show had an agreement that they could give two weeks' notice if they felt they could do something better. Welk wouldn't stop them or try to hold them back."

Welk's well-known procedure in paying scale is dismissed by Norma Zimmer, who argues, "I know that a lot of people were unhappy because he paid scale, but who doesn't pay scale? If they wanted bigger wages, they should have fought with the unions."

Far less publicized—and far more important—is Welk's profit-sharing and bonus system that benefits every employee with his organization. As wardrobe supervisor Rose Weiss states, "I don't know any musician who's been able to walk away with as much money as they all have through profit-sharing. True, he paid scale but he made it up in other ways. One thing that Lawrence did was give bonuses." Another bonus was provided by Dodge during the years they sponsored the show. According to Gus Thow, "Everybody in the band and the singers got a new Dodge every year. For six years all we paid was the license and the insurance."

Prop man Eddie Holland reveals, "Lawrence had a retirement fund for the Musical Family which ended up to be quite a lump of money when they left the show. He always said, 'Musicians don't know how to save their money so I'll save it for them!'"

George Cates on the same issue regarding band members: "The show was on fifty-two weeks a year. There are no musicians in the business who have a show that pays them fifty-two weeks a year. During the summer, there were eight weeks of repeats that everyone got paid for and they got to go out on tour which they got paid for separately. Welk is the *only* bandleader in the business who had a profit-sharing plan for the guys in the band. Everyone who worked for Welk is on profit-sharing, whether you're a secretary, saxophonist, arranger, or vocalist. It was set up with the Treasury Department to make people want to stay. There's also a pension fund."

Each of Welk's employees receives a percentage of his or her total annual salary as his share of the profits, shares that have reportedly amounted to well over one hundred thousand dollars for some of the long-time band members and performers.

Certainly, what put the profit in the profit-sharing was the continuing popularity of the show itself. Jack O'Brien in the *New York Journal-American* intelligently and fairly attempted to analyze Welk's amazing success and the intensely loyal audience of "The Lawrence Welk Show," observing: "Lawrence Welk does not coincide with our taste in popular music, but that schism has never left us disgruntled. We have been enormously 'gruntled' in fact that Welk's lively square sounds have found their own large and devoted millions, and far from suspecting or suggesting that these Welk partisans are wrong, we only maintain they are different. It is our personal concept (in some cases, personal knowledge) that Welk fans range widely in many income brackets. If they have a common denominator, we'd say it's an attraction to folks who have never bothered to pay steady exploratory attention to modern popular music sounds and trends or to musically progressive values. There's nothing wrong with folks who dig Welk. They're not imbeciles, they're not always even squares, even if the Saturday Welkin ringing strikes us as somewhat four-cornered or eight. A lot of Welk admirers would consider us in many spheres of their influence or confluence to be squares indeed. We know a few scientists who consider Welk to be what we insist Duke Ellington, Neal Hefti, the Elgarts, Modern Jazz Quartet, etc., etc. are. In fact, some Welkphiles are far more feverish Champagne Music fans than anyone might suspect is possible. Joseph P. Kennedy, father of a president and of three U.S. senators, a man of many sprightly enthusiasms, was one of Lawrence Welk's earliest TV fans. Back when the Welk show was considered a not-too-permanent summer fill-in, Ambassador Kennedy was singing its praises to us.

"We were resistant, if not insistently, to Joseph P.'s stubborn loyalty to Welk's programs. They did give us a small opportunity to see what made as rich a man as Joseph P. Kennedy take time to admire, and in a spectacularly small way, to help.

"Welk hadn't been on the TV air nearly so securely in those days. Our only peripheral complaint about the Ambassador's expanding admiration was that it delayed the start of the Saturday evening movie; because Joseph P. would insist upon seeing the Welk show before the start of the movie, we had to wait. It became a good-natured weekly argument we knew we would inevitably have to lose. Welk was growing bigger than our aural resistance

The ladies line up to dance with the Maestro during a dress rehearsal. (Courtesy Don Keck)

to his ricky-ticky Mickey Mouse rhythms and sounds. Joseph P. Kennedy did more than donate his attention each Saturday evening. One day he took his pen in hand, signed several checks, then dictated a letter to the president of Chrysler Corporation. In it, he explained he never had bought nor even driven a Dodge station wagon in his considerable lifetime. But he was buying this little motorized wagon train for the Kennedy compound at Hyannis Port, Mass., solely because he had received much pleasure from "The Lawrence Welk Show."

"There is no telling how much this meant to the Welk show at option time. We would guess a lot."

By the mid-1960s, Lawrence Welk had truly become part of America's consciousness, leading one critic to write, "Though no one has kept count of how many

"You may be sure that he has supplied many a comedian with a laugh line." (Courtesy George Thow Collection)

punch lines have been created at Welk's expense, you may be sure he has supplied many a comedian with a laugh line." Indeed, Lawrence Welk was parodied, imitated, and occasionally lampooned—but the basis of this undoubtedly was Welk's great popularity, along with his distinct personality. Like him or not, Lawrence Welk simply had become a show business phenomenon and truly one of a kind.

Reflecting the amazing fortunes of "The Lawrence Welk Show" year after year were the decisions to add a few more cast members, to telecast the program in color, and to tape the show, rather than broadcast live. Although Welk vigorously worked to maintain the exciting "live" feeling of the show by stopping tape only when absolutely necessary, and by taping it in the actual time of sixty minutes, what would be omitted were the often embarrassing mishaps that occurred during a live broadcast.

The first color telecast [the 1965 season premiere] was taped entirely on location at Welk's resort area, Escondido, which is north of San Diego, California. Not only was the show well received, it was also shrewdly effective as promotion for Welk's commercial real estate venture.

Welk proved himself to be something of a television pioneer as it was he who championed that his program be broadcast in color. He was so convinced that color was vital to "The Lawrence Welk Show"'s longevity that he gambled everything—and won.

His battle began when ABC announced the programs to be seen in color for the 1965–66 season and "The Lawrence Welk Show" was *not* one of them. Compounding Welk's consternation was the fact that the network placed one color broadcast before and after the Welk show. Welk announced to Matthew Rosenhaus [president of the J. B. Williams Company, the show's primary sponsor], "If I'm not in color this fall, I may decide not to go on the air at all. I predict that by December, fourteen to twenty percent of the homes in this country will have color sets."

Welk then had Sam Lutz and Don Fedderson meet with ABC executives in New York while he personally telephoned network president Thomas W. Moore. Welk stated that he wanted to cancel the upcoming season, offering to do a few specials instead. Welk's intent was clear: He was perfectly willing to end the show rather than continue broadcasting it in black and white, insisting on complete control as he had done before when others had demanded comedians and dancing girls.

ABC President Moore argued that the Welk show was so popular it did not need the added enticement—and expense—of color telecasts, but Welk was unwilling to relent. ABC notified Welk on July 26 that "The Lawrence Welk Show" would be broadcast in color for the entire 1965–66 season.

The switch in broadcasting the series from black and white to color necessitated some lo-

> *"When Mr. Welk went into a meeting, instead of saying, 'We're going to put our cards on the table,' he said, 'Alright, let's all get in there and put our tables on the floor!'"*
>
> **—KATHY LENNON**

gistical changes. As George Cates explains, "When we went to color, ABC took over the Hollywood Palace and renovated it to be a color studio. We were there a couple of years until they redid the studios down at Prospect and Talmadge for color. Then we moved back to ABC." Cates adds, "It was very hard for us at the Palace because the stage wasn't large enough to have a production area. So the band would be in the back and we'd have a drop, like in the old vaudeville days. It was very difficult."

The Hollywood Palace at Hollywood and Vine Streets in 1965, the temporary and unsatisfactory new home of "The Lawrence Welk Show." (Courtesy Wally Stanard)

The Maestro is saluted on his ten-year network anniversary. (Courtesy Don Keck)

Ron Bacon was promoted from stage manager to assistant director in 1965 and learned then how well-structured the Welk organization was in producing the show, even with the new taping schedule and broadcasting in color—*and* all at a new, unsatisfactory location. "Jim Hobson had a sense of organization that was incredible. He found ways of getting things done very efficiently. The whole Welk organization is that way—Mr. Welk himself and all the people on his staff. He has a very tight, small group of people who do an awful lot of work. For example, he took over a number of publishing companies which had huge buildings full of people. Welk just got rid of all of them and had one or two people running the entire thing. It wasn't necessary to have all those people going out to lunch and sending each other memos. Welk is extremely efficient about things and that makes his organization extremely effective."

The new taping schedule was a model of simplicity and professionalism. Bacon supported Welk's credo that the program was still viewed by everyone as a live performance; also, tape was stopped only when absolutely necessary and, more often than not, nothing interfered with the show's running smoothly. Ron Bacon details the week's production schedule: "The staff had a meeting a week ahead of time, usually on Wednesday. They would plan the production for the next week's show. That meant arrangements had to be made, et cetera. On Thursday, they

Larry Hooper and Jim Roberts acting childishly. (Courtesy Don Keck)

would go to prerecording for certain parts of the music that had to be prerecorded, like background music for some of the elaborate sets where you couldn't get a microphone in there. It was minimal, but there was some of it. All the numbers in the show were rehearsed and they would run down the arrangements. On that same Thursday, they would discuss the sets and production for the following week's show. Then Monday, they would come in and rehearse on a 'dry' stage while the sets were being put up. Then Tuesday, we would tape the show straight through. We would do the show with about ten minutes of rehearsal for each number and we would have a run-through. Then we would break and come back and do the show live [in front of a studio audience]. We always started at exactly eight o'clock and rarely got out of there later than nine-thirty."

Bacon continues, "Generally, we would tape the show all the way through and then would do some pick-up shots and corrections if we had any really deficient areas in the show. Usually there were very few edits. We didn't usually change the audio content of the show. I did one edit which was kind of remarkable. I cut a high note that Kate Smith hit wrong on "God Bless America." She went way sharp, then dropped into it. So we took out about four bars of where she went sharp."

As Bacon remembers, Welk was very much opposed to prerecording, which he felt detracted from the "live" feeling of the program. "He wanted live performances," Bacon says. "He pushed for the live band. I must say, when we got away from that, the shows got dull. He would get us back on course again. He didn't care how much he had to simplify the show to make it work that way.

He wanted a live sound." Music arranger Joe Rizzo reaffirms this. "Lawrence didn't like prerecording. He said, 'You try to fool the people, but they know it's a prerecording.'"

Opinions vary among the cast members, but Myron Floren reveals that when the live broadcasts ended, "It changed quite a bit for me even though it was treated like a live show and taped in front of a live audience. There is something about putting a show on tape, you feel kind of let down, actually. I think it's like making a record. We can go over and over a passage until we get it right; it's just a matter of erasing tape. But when you're doing the show live, you know it's your one chance and if you don't do it right *now*, that's it!"

"One time, Jim Roberts had a fly land right on his nose. He was singing 'Faith Unlocks the Door' and every time he sang the title, he'd hit this fly off his nose. It was live, what else can you do?"

—KATHY LENNON

Myron was more fortunate than most in avoiding the disasters that live television can transmit over the coast-to-coast airwaves, explaining, "Occasionally, I'd completely draw a blank on something I was playing. All of a sudden, you'd realize that this is the last chance I've got to do this. In most cases, from practicing something so much, your fingers and reflexes take over and by the time you remember again, you still haven't made any mistakes."

Lawrence with guest star Kate Smith in 1971.
(Courtesy Don Keck)

"Sometimes, we'd use animals on the show. We were live and they brought a cow out on the set and she relieved herself right next to me as I was singing and it was splashing up right on my gown!"

—NORMA ZIMMER

Joe Rizzo remembers Welk's philosophy regarding mistakes seen on the air. "Bob Lido was great for leaving out a lyric. He would put in a word that fit and nobody ever knew the difference. If you made a real bad mistake, then he'd stop the tape. But he didn't like to stop. He said, nobody's perfect and people like to see things like that."

Bob Ralston states everyone was told that "it cost five thousand dollars every time the tape stopped" and believes that the show was better off recorded in that manner. "I think that kept the spontaneity of the show after we went to tape. Very rarely did we ever take more than sixty minutes to tape a sixty-minute show."

Rudy Horvatich illustrates how Lawrence's own routine was just as regimented as the program itself. "The show was taped on Tuesday, as regular as it could possibly be, taped between eight and nine o'clock. Dress rehearsal was 5:30 to 6:30. Then Lawrence would come in, lie down, have something to eat, and relax. I would make him up and then he would go out and meet his audience. Lawrence had a huge dressing room which included a bathroom with a mirror and lights where we'd do his makeup."

Rudy continues, "I would make him up in time to get on stage and he would address his fans. He always had Myron and a few of the guys from the band who were already made up perform for them. There was always that happy feeling and Lawrence always had that smile on his face. In between numbers he and the cue card man would go over what he had to say. Lawrence always added the finishing touches to everything.

Myron Floren in duck soup as Harpo Marx.
(Courtesy Don Keck)

72

"I do know he had his fears," reveals Rudy, speaking of Welk's constant desire to please his audience. "He showed so much concentration for every show that he wanted perfection and he usually got it. He was wise enough, or fortunate enough, to know that a good show could only be put on by having the best musicians around that were available and who could live in a family-like atmosphere such as he had. 'The Lawrence Welk Show' was truly a family affair. I'm amazed at all the good musicians he has put together in one band. For all the years I have known them, I have never seen any arguments between the band members. They got along so well that I couldn't believe it. Musicians are naturally complex, intelligent, and sensitive and [as such] could be very uptight. But his people never did show it. They also had a wonderful feeling among them and I think he was indeed fortunate, or he had the wisdom to put the right people together."

"Lawrence knew that I started out as a musician. I was sitting in the back of a car we were driving to a location to shoot and the radio was playing. I began to hum and then my humming went into a little singing. Lawrence, sitting in the front, turned around and said, "Rudy, don't quit your job as a makeup man!"

—RUDY HORVATICH

As Welk once remarked, "We've always had that wonderful friendliness in our group. One of the things that astonishes others in the world of entertainment is the lack of jealousy among our people. Oh, of course, there's a little—there's bound to be—that's just human nature."

Cissy King and Jo Ann Castle giving paws to Art Duncan's Easter egg. (Courtesy Don Keck)

Art Duncan.
(Courtesy George Thow
Collection)

Proof of the wisdom of Welk's work ethic and his ability to maintain that family feeling within the ever-growing Welk organization was that the show was able to continue smoothly through the many cast changes that occurred over the next several years.

One addition to the Musical Family who has remained with the show to the present was dancer Arthur Duncan, who joined in 1964. At the time of his first appearance on "The Lawrence Welk Show" in January of that year, Duncan was performing in Los Angeles with Lionel Hampton. Arthur so dazzled Welk's audience that fan mail poured in, wanting to see more of Duncan's fancy footwork that led to his second appearance three weeks later. Soon after, Arthur Duncan

was invited by Welk to become a permanent member and, importantly, the first black performer on "The Lawrence Welk Show."

No stranger to television, Duncan had toured the globe and appeared on an Australian television program for over a year (where he met singer Ken Delo, who hosted the show and who would join the Welk Musical Family himself in 1969). Art returned to America and did many guests shots on programs starring Jerry Lewis, Bob Hope, Jimmy Durante, and Red Skelton.

Lawrence Welk praised the fine dancer by stating, "Arthur Duncan is the man who is keeping the art of tap dancing alive in this country, and is one of the finest gentlemen I know."

74

"Meeting Mr. Welk was the most wonderful event of my entire life!" proclaimed Natalie Nevins about her years on "The Lawrence Welk Show" (1965–69). An accomplished vocalist who also played the piano and flute, Natalie reveals her joy of performing, saying, "All I can ever think of is standing still and singing and having people enjoy hearing me. To me, that's all there is."

Natalie Nevins.
(Courtesy Don Keck)

75

Audience favorite Aladdin. (Courtesy Don Keck)

For quite different reasons, several beloved members of Welk's Musical Family would depart by 1968: Aladdin Pallante, Barbara Boylan, and the Lennon Sisters.

Aladdin's decision to leave the show was triggered by a severe heart attack that caused his absence from the program for several weeks. At the time Aladdin said, "The illness made me realize how important it is to get as much out of living as you can. If there's something you've always wanted to do, don't procrastinate. There might not be a tomorrow."

Welk was deeply saddened by Aladdin's departure and said, "I never thought he'd do it. I'm sorry to see him go. But we had many wonderful years together and I know Aladdin is doing what is right for him. I wish him all the best and I'm sure we'll always be the best of friends."

Barbara Boylan chose to retire from show business at a young age to be a full-time wife and mother. "I met my husband, Greg Dixon, on the show," explains Barbara. "He was a singer with the Blenders, and when we met, boy, that was it! It got to be that Bobby [Burgess] and I were traveling so much we were living out of a plane, practically. I realized it was too difficult to have a successful marriage and to keep going at that pace."

The Blenders were a group of four college boys who signed in their sophomore year to join the show in its 1965 season. Eventually, three of the members chose to leave show business and red-headed Steve Smith remained to sing what was referred to then as the "young" songs. Steve also managed to obtain his college degree during the four years he appeared on the program, an accomplishment in which Welk took great pride.

The Blenders. (Courtesy Don Keck)

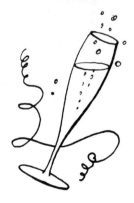

Bobby and Barbara on location at Escondido.
(Courtesy Don Keck)

Did Barbara regret her decision to leave "The Lawrence Welk Show" and a show business career? "I knew it was the right choice," Barbara says firmly. "I hadn't had a break, a vacation, or a weekend off in five years. My honeymoon was my first vacation. My vacations had always been Lake Tahoe, but we did two shows a night and three on Saturday and that was supposed to be our vacation! But it was a great opportunity and I loved Mr. Welk. He was super to me."

Welk and Barbara had a close, paternal relationship and Barbara repaid his interest with great dedication. Welk had instilled in her his "show must go on" professionalism and Barbara recalls that once, during a live broadcast, "I ruined my ankle and I was really pretty hurt but I had to go back on. Of course, if it [the show] were taped, I wouldn't have had to. But I went on and did another number and went right to the hospital."

Barbara Boylan is serenaded by Aladdin and friends at her farewell party, June 6, 1967. (Courtesy Don Keck)

Boylan views Lawrence as a "warm, loving father. I really cared and he appreciated it. I remember when I left he wrote me a beautiful letter and it was from his heart."

The last night Barbara was on the show, Welk asked her to say something to all the folks while saying farewell. Barbara burst into tears and wailed, "I just can't! If I do, I'll just keep crying like this! Oh, I don't want to go!"

Time has not altered Barbara Boylan's love of her days on "The Lawrence Welk Show." "We were all really close as a family," she fondly recalls, adding, "Those were my good years. I treasure those moments."

"At the end of a New Year's Eve performance at the Hollywood Palladium, Lawrence Welk noticed the throngs of bus tour senior-citizen guests all heading out the doors at two minutes past midnight. Later telling the story, Lawrence explained, "The people left in groves!"

—MYRON FLOREN

The Lennon Sisters literally grew up before America's eyes since their first appearance on "The Lawrence Welk Show" in December 1955. Lawrence and his audience immediately took the Lennons to their hearts, all becoming deeply involved in their personal and professional lives.

Kathy Lennon admits that eldest sister Dianne's decision to leave the family act in 1960 to get married was "quite traumatic. Aside from getting married and moving out, she was also leaving the group in which she was the lead. She was the solo singer, the one who took care of all of us on the road. It was a big decision that Dianne had to make. In fact, she made it about four or five times, because every time she went to Mr. Welk, he'd say, 'Well, we'll work something out.' So, Dianne would go to Daddy, who'd say, 'Well, we'll see when the time comes.' Dee Dee [Dianne]'s husband, Dick, said, 'It's up to you,' and she said 'I want to be a housewife and I want a big family. That's all I ever wanted to do.' The four of us were raised to feel that way. We had an incredible example because Mom and Dad are two very special people. That made it work and it was a happy home, and that's all we wanted. So when Dee Dee left, Janet went through a big change, because here she was, the little one, and she had to carry the lead. It was the most intricate part in the group and she didn't know if she could do it. But the support was there from all of us—the Welk band, Mr. Welk, and Daddy. And it worked."

The girls wondered at this time, as Kathy Lennon now reveals, whether their popularity would "go down when Dee Dee left." On the contrary, they soon discovered "we traveled *more*. At one point, we were traveling nine months out of the year. We'd come home on weekends, do the television show, and fly back out. We were gone an awful lot. We played every club, every state fair, and every variety television show. Whatever show was on we performed on it!"

The Lennon Sisters mature.
(Courtesy Kathy Lennon)

"In 1964," continues Kathy, "Dee Dee's husband, who worked for the telephone company, went on strike for a year. Dee Dee had adopted her first child and was expecting her second. Mr. Welk heard this and said, 'Since he's on strike and I'm sure you need a little help, why don't you come back and sing on the show? You don't have to go on the road trips. So Dee Dee came back. Then Peggy got married and started having her babies. Dee Dee would fill in for Peggy and then Janet married and had *her* babies and pretty soon it evolved back to the four of us and it has been the four of us ever since."

As the sisters matured, "We felt we had to grow with the music and the sound," says Kathy Lennon. "And we wanted to grow up too and not be put in that little box of four little girls singing with the accordion." This, says Kathy, was part of "what led to our break with Lawrence Welk."

"There were times we had conflict. We'd want to do something more contemporary. Welk would say, 'Well, our people wouldn't understand that,' and we'd go back and do 'Moonlight Bay' or whatever. There were a few times when we really bumped heads and it was very difficult for us because we didn't want to make waves. And yet, we also wanted to grow with the music. In the later years, Mr. Welk did add a lot of contemporary songs that were done in his style, his way. But when we were with him, he would fight against that.

"We'd show him a new song and he'd say, 'Do you think that the housewives who are doing the dishes can walk away after hearing that and hum it?'" Kathy remembers, to which the girls would reply, "'Maybe not.' Then he would say the number couldn't be on the show. Mr. Welk knew they had to keep it in their heads and say, wasn't that a nice little tune. That's why he toured so much. He found out what the public wanted and used it on the show."

Why did the Lennon Sisters leave "The Lawrence Welk Show"? The reasons were clear to Kathy Lennon, who says, "We had decided that we could make a lot more money and spend a lot more time with our families if we left the Welk show and also grow with the music. It's very important to do a variety of songs. I think Mr. Welk's concept of his show was unique and wonderful and it proved to be the most successful television show ever, when it comes to the numbers of years on the air. But we had to go on with our lives and this was the way of not working four days a week, which we were doing fifty-two weeks of the year, and instead work eight weeks out of the year and make four times the amount of money. It was the only decision to make, and when we were all married that was the decision we made. We went on to do our own television show with Jimmy Durante for a year and then we became guests on "The Andy Williams Show" for a year; we were on every other week. Then we continued to do state fair and concert dates and Las Vegas. And we work now, maybe seven weeks of the year."

What is not generally known is that the Lennon Sisters had the opportunity to leave the show many years before when executive producer Don Fedderson approached the girls to star in a new situation comedy series he was to produce called "My Three Daughters," a distaff version of what would become "My Three Sons," one of television's longest running series (1960–72). "At the time," says Kathy, "we went to Mr. Welk and said 'Our commitment is to you.' We were also asked a few times to do the beach party movies and an Elvis Presley film. At the time, our Dad didn't feel it was good for our reputation and he declined. Looking back now, it probably would have been a wonderful thing for us although maybe it would have hurt our image and lost a lot of our audience. Another time we were approached to do a musical version of *Little Women*, but they weren't able to clear the rights. We had comic books, coloring books and paper dolls and magic slates. There were many Lennon Sisters products and we made good money off of those."

By 1967 the Lennon Sisters had made a firm decision to leave "The Lawrence Welk Show." Kathy reveals, "We went through a hard time then because Mr. Welk was very hurt when we left. So were we. It was a big change for us. We were leaving our family. Mr. Welk was not pleased that we left, but at the end, he was the one that let us go. We saw Mr. Welk a few times after that and it was always hugs and kisses, but underneath, he was hurt and so were we. But it [the decision] had to be made. It's like a child leaving his parents."

Kathy Lennon credits Welk with saying soon after the break, "Since the Lennon Sisters left my show, they've been digging their own funerals." Yet publicly, Welk maintained an attitude of acceptance and understanding reflected in the comments printed in a fan magazine published shortly after the highly publicized "divorce" between Dianne, Peggy, Kathy, and Janet Lennon and Lawrence Welk. In that magazine (published with Welk's cooperation), it was reported, "The girls were with Lawrence a dozen years, and most of them were happy. But during 1967 the girls began to get increasingly unhappy. They wanted to do other shows and relegate the Welk show to something they could do at their own convenience. They had always been free to do any other show in addition to the Welk performance, and they had earned a great deal of money under that arrangement. But now, they felt they wanted more freedom.

"Lawrence could not arrange things for them as they wished. He is completely honorable in his business arrangements, as in everything else, and he had promised his sponsors and the network a full Welk show each week and obviously a Lawrence Welk show would include the Lennon Sisters. There was also a fine line of behavior to be drawn for the other performances. If each performer wanted to do the show only on the basis of his or her choice, the show would soon disintegrate. It was an insoluble dilemma. And since the Lennons would not agree to stay on a permanent basis, and Lawrence could not have them performing only at times they wished, their long and happy association came to an end.

"It was sad. They had truly become part of each other's life. Lawrence, in a very real way had made these girls a household word, had established them as the whole nation's little sisters, had given them an identity that no one else could have done. They, in turn, had given him the unique sweetness and freshness that distinguished them during those years, so although the parting was bittersweet, it ended as do all of Lawrence's associations, with good instead of ill feelings.

"The Lennons and the Welks still see each other. 'I wish the girls only the best,' says Lawrence. 'I hope they will be even more successful. I always feel it's a feather in my cap when some of my performers go on to bigger things and I wish the girls every success.'"

Reflecting the feelings of sisters Dianne, Peggy, and Janet, Kathy Lennon says admiringly of her former boss, "He's an incredible musician and has an incredible ear. He has an ear for talent. He knows how to build talent. He knows how to get a reaction. He still has an audience out there that wants to hear him. He would make us stay after concerts and we would sign autographs for hours, for anybody who was there. They had come all the way from such and such a place to see us and it was important to him that we did. We respect him and hold him in high regard in many ways."

Two female vocalists joined the program in 1967 and gave the show a country flavor, but

"When Lawrence Welk heard of a politician who was being lauded for some charitable deed, he commented, 'That's a real feather in his head.'"

—MYRON FLOREN

both Andrea Willis and Lynn Anderson would be with "The Lawrence Welk Show" for only a short period of time.

Andrea Willis specialized in country-pop tunes and left the show in 1969 without any of the notoriety that surrounded the departure of the Lennons. Reportedly, Andrea exited—whether it was her choice or not is unknown—to spend more time with her family, not wanting to travel extensively on the road tours. (Norma Zimmer had also made

Lynn Anderson and the band. (Courtesy Don Keck)

84

the same decision not to tour in order to raise her teenaged sons, with Welk's approval). When first hired, Andrea was heralded as a replacement of sorts for the Lennon Sisters.

Lynn Anderson, who would become one of country music's most popular recording artists, joined the Welk group for only one year. Though extremely popular with viewers and well-liked by the cast, Lynn left the show to be with her husband, who was a music publisher in Nashville, and also to focus on her career as a solo performer. Her choice was a wise one, as evidenced by her country classic best-seller "I Never Promised You a Rose Garden."

The one remaining addition to the 1967–68 season, a necessary one, was a dance partner for Bobby Burgess to replace happily married and now retired Barbara Boylan Dixon.

Bobby details his search for Barbara's successor: "I put an ad in the trades [*Variety* and *The Hollywood Reporter*], stressing someone with a theater arts background who really knew ballroom [dancing]. I auditioned about thirty girls over four or five months." Bobby then remembered that another dancer, John King, had a sister named Cissy and learned that she was visiting from Albuquerque, New Mexico, to enter a dance contest in Los Angeles. Bobby arranged an audition and concluded Cissy King was "the right height, the right weight, and the right look."

Another kind of partner came into Bobby Burgess's life at that time: Myron Floren's daughter, Kristie. "I had known her since she was nine," says Bobby. "There is a ten-year difference in our ages. I would always go around and say 'hi' to the kids on the Christmas shows. Kristie studied ballet, so I'd go up to her and say, 'How are you doing with your dancing?' She was real shy, but real cute. When Barbara left, I took my waterski boat up to Lake Tahoe and I went over to Emerald Bay, and there was Kristie and her sister. Kristie had changed! We dated for about two years until she was nineteen and I was twenty-nine. We got married and have

three kids. A lot of romances bloomed on that show. Some didn't last, but a lot of them did."

Cissy King would last ten years as Bobby Burgess's dancing partner and was well-suited to the job. "Cissy had been a gymnast," says Bobby, "so she did the lifts very well. Plus, she studied what they called international modern dance—and her blond hair is a contrast to mine."

"I've danced all my life," says Cissy King. "It started when I was about two but I didn't get serious about it until I was about two and a half. I knew it was for me. I had all kinds of training: ballet, tap, and acrobatics. When I was eleven, I was taking the bus down to the YMCA with records and record player in hand, teaching classes. I was earning money as a dance teacher, teaching kids my age and older. I started ballroom dancing at the time I was eight and then entered various dance competitions.

"Bobby saw me in a dance contest in Los Angeles at Thanksgiving of 1966. Barbara was engaged to be married and Bobby was keeping his eye open for talent. He was judging the ballroom contest and saw me dancing and came over and introduced himself and asked to dance with me. He asked me to audition the next day and then a few months later, he asked me to do the show when Barbara was away on her honeymoon."

Cissy does not recall encountering any difficulties in joining the show as another dancer's replacement. "I was a totally different look," Cissy notes. "With the Welk show, you have to concentrate on the show and traveling and show business and so I knew that Bobby didn't have time to keep up with what was going on in the world of competitive and technical dancing, so I knew I had all that to contribute.

"I made an agreement with Bobby that for a full year, we would do all new numbers and establish ourselves as a team, rather than doing anything that was Bobby and Barbara's," remembers Cissy, who states that

Bobby and his new partner, Cissy King.
(Courtesy George Thow Collection)

Cissy and Bobby salute St.
Patrick's Day by the
wearin' of the green.
(Courtesy George Thow
Collection)

Bobby's change in partners met with easy acceptance. "I only received one negative letter in all the years on the show," she says.

Cissy, however, remembers a severe negative reaction to her television debut—her own. "The first time I was on TV we had a whole group of people over to the house for a celebration. Then came a close-up of me on camera and I felt I looked cross-eyed and I screamed!"

Cissy King soon found her own unique way of communicating with Lawrence on what the dance team wanted to feature each week. "I knew I went in many times as a kind of buffer for us doing something radical like the latest fad dance. I would present it as, 'It's kind of like the Charleston . . . and we would get to do it rather than telling him that we were thinking of doing something very new that the audience wouldn't understand. He understood that we just wanted to show that "The Lawrence Welk Show" knew of those things, that we were aware and current, too."

In the turbulent times of the late 1960s, "The Lawrence Welk Show" remained deliberately unscathed by social unrest, hippies, acid rock music, and distrust of the over-thirty age group that was considered "The Establishment." Such a peculiar time warp did not go unnoticed by viewers and critics alike.

Dick Helm wrote in *Variety* on the Welk phenomenon in 1968: "If the ratings can be taken as a criterion, more people stay home on Saturday night to look and listen to the pride of the Dakotas than for any other admissible reason. And they've been doing it for going on fourteen years to keep the big band sound alive and regale the faithful. From the first day Don Fedderson and Sam Lutz sold the show, sponsorship never wavered. The road ahead looks just as straight and inviting despite Welk's flippancy that 'I've got to take things easier or the government will take away my Social Security and Medicare.' Welk has been reviewed in these pages for every year of his fourteen, so there has been very little unsaid about his success. To nail it down, he's folksy and never puts on, as they say up Dakota way. He has flowery compliments for all his entertainers, and never utters an unkind word. And to cap it all, there are millions who say, 'He'll put on a darn good show each week.' His sponsors must think so too . . . what producer-director Jim Hobson and Sam Lutz stage every week is a potpourri of earthy entertainment. No comics nor acrobats, just music and songs by attractive people. . . . As had been said about Bob Hope, he never gives a bad show; some are just better than others. And this goes for Welk, too; or why would the viewers keep coming back in such numbers to keep [the show] in the Nielsen Top 20 for nearly all his years? Charisma, perhaps, but showmanship to be sure."

Cissy and Bobby cutting a rug. (Courtesy Don Keck)

"Nobody's going to pull the wool over my head!"

—**LAWRENCE WELK**

Three singers became new regulars in the 1968 season: Tanya Falan and the duo of Sandi [Jensen] and Salli [Flynn]. While Salli would leave the show in 1972 and later marry Welk musician Clay Hart (who joined the series that same year), Sandi remained until 1980.

Tanya Falan in 1968.
(Courtesy Don Keck)

88

Salli's future husband,
Welk discovery Clay Hart.
(Courtesy George Thow Collection)

Sandi and Salli.
(Courtesy Don Keck)

"Salli warmed him up. He was 'Mr. Welk' before that. Salli would just go up and squeeze him and say, 'Lawrence, oh, how are you?' He responded so much to it that it got to the point where all the girls did the same. Lawrence loved the attention."

—CISSY KING

Mary Lee Schaefer, president of the Lawrence Welk Fan Club, heard a young vocalist named Tanya Falan perform at Disneyland and brought her to Welk's attention. Welk was so captivated that he invited Tanya to appear on his New Year's Eve program of 1967. As always, Lawrence's instinct in discovering new talent was corroborated by tremendous audience response, and Tanya became a new member of the Musical Family and a viewer favorite. (Tanya also soon became a part of Lawrence Welk's "real" family when she married Larry Welk, Jr., the following year. Before they divorced, Tanya and Larry presented Lawrence and wife, Fern, with two grandchildren, Lawrence Welk, III ("Buns"), and younger son Kevin.)

The team of Sandi and Salli ushered in the beginning of the later, somewhat more contemporary generation; the girls also began addressing the Maestro as "Lawrence" rather than the customary "Mr. Welk."

Welk discovered Salli and Sandi when they competed with two hundred other young singers at an open audition at the Hollywood Palladium. Lawrence was quickly taken with the two talented young women and invited them to the ABC studios the next day to sing for his production staff. In short order, Sandi and Salli made their first appearance on "The Lawrence Welk Show."

The girls first met as students at Brigham Young University in Utah at a school audition. "It was just as if I'd suddenly acquired a sister," said Salli. "We found we liked the same things, the same people, and the same boys, and we've become fast friends since that time. We have so much in common that it seems like we actually are sisters. Everything just seemed to take a natural course once we met each other."

That course took them to Disneyland where, like Tanya Falan, they performed for a time, which led to a contract with Capitol Records. In 1967, Sandi and Salli went on a USO tour of Viet Nam and later that year appeared at Harrah's Club in Lake Tahoe with headliner Jack Jones; their audition with Welk came directly after that engagement.

Mail poured in after that first appearance and as a result, Lawrence asked the girls on camera after their third appearance to become permanent members of the Musical Family, which was a complete surprise to the duo.

In 1969, the year Salli met her future husband Clay Hart on the show, Sandi married her college sweetheart Brent Griffiths, and would take his name professionally.

Welk was quite enthused about his newest discoveries, saying at the time, "Nothing can stop these two girls. If they continue to handle themselves the way they have been, and work as hard as they always have, they'll go right to the top—and stay there!"

Art Duncan and Ken Delo.
(Courtesy George Thow Collection)

Another singer who went right to the top of Welk popularity was Ken Delo, who joined "The Lawrence Welk Show" in 1969 after auditioning for Sam Lutz. By coincidence, Ken Delo had hosted the Australian television program on which Arthur Duncan had appeared for thirteen months in the early 1960s. Welk considered Ken a triple threat— he could sing, dance, and act, all with the Welk style and flair. Ken quickly discovered his ability to charm the ladies of the studio audience when he would frequently serenade them as he moved through the aisles. Ken Delo is unquestionably a Welk fixture and has not broken his association with Lawrence Welk since his debut on the show.

Jo Ann and Myron play dueling keyboards. (Courtesy Don Keck)

Two departures from "The Lawrence Welk Show" in 1969 were due to very different circumstances, but nevertheless attracted equal amounts of publicity: the firing of Natalie Nevins and the friendly parting of Welk and honky-tonk ragtime piano player Jo Ann Castle, who left to pursue a solo career.

Jo Ann's departure was well planned in advance and discussed at length with Welk and, as such, both made the break as smooth as possible. Lawrence has stated that he considers Jo Ann a prime example of someone who worked well with the Welk organization and allowed it to help her, and one who left only good feelings when she departed.

"I didn't have any trouble working for him at all. Most people didn't. If you were there on time, you were good on your instrument, very dependable and you went along with what you felt Lawrence wanted you never had any trouble."

—CHARLOTTE HARRIS

Natalie Nevins's exit by all accounts was quite different from Jo Ann Castle's—she was fired for failing to appear at a concert date in Spokane, Washington. Natalie insisted she was ill and unable to make the performance, but she reportedly did not notify anyone of that fact prior to the concert and was unable to produce a medical statement for corroboration.

Natalie's attempt at a reconciliation—including baking her "famous" blueberry muffins for Lawrence—was unsuccessful, for Welk would not budge on his decision to fire her. Natalie had violated one of his operating credos and to him it was not possible to make amends for what he considered to be highly unprofessional and inexcusable conduct.

Two talented singers who were the last performers to join "The Lawrence Welk Show" during its ABC reign also broke Welk's taboo by becoming the only married couple ever to appear on the program as regulars. Welk praised Guy and Ralna Hovis as "one of the nicest things to ever happen to me," admitting that he felt "goosebumps" when he heard them sing together for the first time.

Natalie Nevins, Joe Feeney, Larry Hooper, Curt Ramsey, and Dick Dale. (Courtesy Don Keck)

Ralna and Guy Hovis. (Courtesy George Thow Collection)

The beginning of the next decade proved to be one of Lawrence Welk's most difficult, but ultimately triumphant, times of his career. More than ever before, "The Lawrence Welk Show" was viewed by many as an anachronism, a curio catering to the old and the unsophisticated. Reflecting this sentiment is a 1970 article that appeared in the *Los Angeles Examiner* by television critic Morton Moss, who wrote: "The youngbloods and their feminine counterparts consider him a quaintly humorous leftover from the age of the dinosaur. But the 'iron-poor bloods' and others on their wavelength find him a beloved shelter from a sliding world whose gyrations elude their comprehension and sympathy."

P. F. Kudge in the *Wall Street Journal* that same year wrote in a similar vein, "While thirteen million American homes are tuned in via ABC-TV to a previously taped episode of Mr. Welk's fifteen-year-old show, four thousand representations of the Welk Nation—as far in spirit from the Woodstock Nation as it is possible to be—are here at the Hollywood Palladium in person. They have come from every corner of the country where Lawrence Welk's music is *the* music and

where Saturday night is his night. The air is heavy with ritual as the band begins with the theme song, 'Bubbles in the Wine.'. . . Lawrence Welk has not amassed all his wealth by heeding the critics, who have dismissed the Welk brand of music as hopelessly square, bland ricky-tick rhythms aimed at a fading generation. This is the kind of music the bandleader likes himself, and he sees in his success undeniable proof that others like it too. He doesn't rail against the new sound; it is just not his thing."

Welk undoubtedly was not immune to such observations or attacks on his "out-of-date" musical tastes and wholesome image, yet he himself admits that only when he even fleetingly catered to those "outside influences" did it jeopardize his enormous popularity and the trust bestowed upon him by the American public who were his fans. "If I had put my foot down more firmly during the last year we appeared on ABC," Welk once remarked, "and insisted on playing the kind of music that was right for us—then we might never have lost our show."

Welk had seen many musical trends come and go, but clearly none of them had the impact of rock 'n' roll. He cared not one bit for

it and felt his audience felt the same way. However, faced with the deluge of this "new" music on the market he began playing it—tailored to his Champagne Music sound, of course—but did so against his better judgment. This turn of events happened largely because of the band members and some of the young performers, who constantly pressured Lawrence into featuring more contemporary songs.

Other changes in television signaled the end of "The Lawrence Welk Show"'s sixteen-year association with the ABC network. The Federal Communications Commission (FCC) handed out a new ruling that reduced network prime-time programming by one half-hour per night, intending to provide smaller stations with more programming muscle. And, for the first time, "The Lawrence Welk Show" lost its time slot of sixteen years and was moved up one hour earlier Saturday nights. As a result, ABC's televised sports events often meant "The Lawrence Welk Show" was delayed an hour or longer, causing further disruption to the show's loyal viewers.

Sam Lutz and Don Fedderson were in constant communication with ABC brass in New York, anxious to learn the fate of what the network once considered its bread-and-butter programming staple; ABC was implementing its new programming strategy, as were the other networks, to seek younger, more affluent viewers. Advertisers felt that the "older" audience was "demographically undesirable" and, following suit, networks were revamping their schedules by wiping out still highly rated programs and catering instead to programs and personalities that would appeal more to younger viewers. It appeared "The Lawrence Welk Show" was tagged as part of ABC's housecleaning.

On Monday, March 11, 1971, ABC told Lutz and Fedderson that the network had made no definite decision concerning the fate of the show. The next day, however, Welk read an industry trade paper that said that his show would "probably" be axed. Frantic calls immediately placed to ABC in New York yielded only the nonresponse that a decision would not be forthcoming until the following week.

On Tuesday, March 19, Welk and his business manager Ted Lennon [uncle of the Lennon Sisters] were in Escondido to play in a golf tournament when Welk was summoned to the phone. The caller was UPI reporter Rick DuBrow, who informed him that "The Lawrence Welk Show" was not on ABC's list of programs for the upcoming fall season that he had just received. "The Lawrence Welk Show" seemed destined soon to become television history.

Heartsick, Lawrence nevertheless managed to weather the next several days of countless telegrams, calls from friends and the press, and viewer mail protesting the show's cancellation. (There were reportedly more than one million pieces of mail delivered to the Welk offices at this time, excluding the huge number sent to ABC stations across the country.) Compounding his discomfort, Lawrence was also suffering from the flu, but went ahead with previously arranged plans for a dinner party with Fern and old and dear friends, including his Dodge mentors Bert and Nancy Carter.

During the dinner, Welk received a long-distance call from Matty Rosenhaus, president of the show's principal sponsor, the J. B. Williams Company. When he returned to the dinner table, Welk emotionally recounted to his guests their conversation, in which Rosenhaus assured him unconditionally that the Williams Company would remain with him in whatever he decided to do. Welk was deluged with so many requests from television stations across the country to continue the program that soon a decision was made to produce the show for syndication.

In less than one week, "The Lawrence Welk Show" rose from the ashes and the Lawrence Welk Television Network was born.

"On a flight to Dallas, our Electra prop-jet was tossed and buffeted about during a violent thunderstorm and battered by hurricane-force winds. When we finally came to a very rocky landing, Lawrence turned to me and said, 'For a second there, I saw my whole life pass between my eyes!'"

—MYRON FLOREN

The creation of the Lawrence Welk Network proved to be one of Welk's most satisfying accomplishments. In short order, "The Lawrence Welk Show" proved itself stronger than ever as it became apparent that it would now be seen on *more* stations in syndication than it had during its sixteen-year ABC network run! Local ABC stations—110 of them—stood in line to carry "The Lawrence Welk Show," a situation that was then duplicated by local CBS and NBC affiliates, which also picked up the show for their stations. Including independent stations, the Welk Net-

"Ah-one, ah-two . . ."
(Courtesy George Thow Collection)

work began with a healthy 168 markets and mushroomed into a record 261 stations soon after.

While George Cates states syndication "wasn't a difficult transition," Rudy Horvatich reveals that ABC's cancellation affected Welk deeply. "That really hurt him, because we had become family at ABC. He thought that ABC didn't want him any more. He really wanted to come back in his old time slot on the network."

Rudy adds that even though the financial gains were greater for Welk in syndication, Lawrence cared most about staying on the air for his loyal following. "Even though it was making more money for him at the time, I

don't think Lawrence was ever in there for the money. I think he was there because he loved being on the air, he loved his fans, and he loved to appear on as many one-night engagements as he could: just for the purpose that his fans would get to see him."

Horvatich continues, "I know he looked forward every week to the show. We discussed that many times during the makeup sessions and he never had the feeling of not wanting to come to the show. I know he did the show when he was feeling bad physically because of a cold he couldn't get rid of, but yet, throughout the years, he never faded. You can certainly be proud of a person like that."

Gail Farrell, Sandi Griffiths,
and Mary Lou Metzger.
(Courtesy George Thow Collection)

Reflecting on Lawrence Welk's longevity and continuing popularity, Alfred G. Aronowitz wrote in the *New York Post* in 1971: "He's a nice old man, Lawrence Welk, who likes to keep things plain and simple just like he was taught down on the farm in Strasburg, North Dakota. He didn't really learn how to speak English until he packed up and left for the big city . . . poor, plain and simple Lawrence. He still talks like he just stepped off the boat . . . and all he ever learned was how to make money.

"They call him the 'Corn Belt Guy Lombardo' and the 'Liberace of the Accordion.'

Whatever else they call him, he's such a nice old man that it's hard to dislike him even if he was the one to force the Sid Caesar show off the air. Lawrence knows about ratings. He used to carry an applause meter on tour with him but now his ear has gotten so finely attuned that he doesn't need any mechanical help in telling him whether he's going over or not.

"He'll be sixty-nine next March and he's still touring. He was in Roanoke, Virginia, the other day when he called me up to hustle his appearance in Madison Square Garden. . . . They've 'only' sold 14,000 tickets out of a possible 20,000."

As of the 1971 television season, Lawrence Welk's Musical Family included performers Dick Dale, Norma Zimmer, Myron Floren, Larry Hooper, Ken Delo, Bob Lido, Buddy Merrill, Jim Roberts, Joe Feeney, Jack Imel, Bobby Burgess and Cissy King, Joe Livoti, Bob Ralston, Arthur Duncan, Tanya Falan Welk, the Hotsy Totsy Boys, Clay Hart, Guy and Ralna, Peanuts Hucko and Salli Flynn (both of whom would leave in 1972), Sandi Jensen, Gail Farrell, Mary Lou Metzger, and Welk's newest discovery, young Mexican vocalist Anacani.

When Salli Flynn left the show, the new vocal trio of Sandi, Gail, and Mary Lou proved very popular. Gail tagged Lawrence to dance one night when he played the Hollywood Palladium and took full advantage of the situation by auditioning for him then and there—in front of the entire Palladium audience. Mary Lou had a more conventional approach, phoning Welk and requesting an audition while she was in Los Angeles for the "College Bowl" television program.

Welk discovered Anacani, his new Mexican sensation, in the restaurant in his resort area, Escondido, where she and her family were dining in hopes of getting her an audition. Anacani stopped Welk as he was leaving the restaurant and she sang for him as the other patrons watched and listened, breaking into applause when she finished. Their response was so spontaneous and enthusiastic that it convinced Welk instantly to feature Anacani on his program.

Mexican sensation Anacani. (Courtesy George Thow Collection)

99

The Hotsy Totsy Boys.
(Courtesy Don Keck)

Welk's Hotsy Totsy Boys were fashioned after his band from years before, with numbers played in the same razzle-dazzle style, thanks to Bob Lido, Charlie Parlato, Russ Klein, Jack Imel, Richard Maloof, Bob Ralston, and Bob Haines.

Every Musical Family member was primed on presenting a first-rate syndication premiere show to be televised on September 9, 1971, and, happily, "The Lawrence Welk Show" never missed a beat. ABC had scheduled summer reruns of the series through the first week of September, so despite its cancellation, "The Lawrence Welk Show" had not missed one week on the air (except the week of President John F. Kennedy's assassination in November 1963) since its network premiere on July 2, 1955. It was a truly remarkable achievement.

To some outsiders, it seemed rather odd that Welk chose to continue taping his syndicated series at ABC after that network had unceremoniously dumped him. Welk insisted that he harbored no ill feelings and instead

*George Cates fronting the band with
the entire company.* (Courtesy Wally Stanard)

voiced his appreciation to ABC for giving him such a long run. His only complaint was losing his old dressing room and being assigned one "about as big as a box." Undaunted, Welk and his team prepared the all-important premiere show.

A theme was chosen. "The Lawrence Welk Show" would salute the Broadway hit musical *No, No Nanette*, Champagne Music–style. Rose Weiss designed all the costumes in blue and white, and the men wore coordinating blue jackets with white flannel slacks. The finishing touch was pale blue chiffon swags placed across the set on each side of the crystal chandeliers, creating a lovely effect.

Bob Warren announced the show, proclaiming, "The Lawrence Welk Network presents—'The Lawrence Welk Show!'"

which led into a new overture composed for the occasion by resident genius George Cates. The show proceeded "wunnerfully" well, without a single hitch; the highlight was the show's capper, a tap dance (choreographed by Jack Imel) by the entire cast to "Tea for Two" gamely attempted by even Joe Feeney, who proved then to be a much better singer than dancer!

Gail and May Lou smell something fishy.
(Courtesy Don Keck)

*Wally Stanard and Lawrence in a pensive
moment on the set.* (Courtesy Wally Stanard)

Despite Welk's creative satisfaction with the premiere, he was quite concerned about the low Neilsen ratings that recorded a viewing audience of 6.2 million, slightly below the sponsor's estimate of 7.5 million. Welk was all the more determined to make this "new" Lawrence Welk series a hit for everyone and became even more deeply involved with music selection and production concept; Welk asked Jim Hobson to include many close-ups of the performers to establish greater, more intimate rapport with the audience.

Changing trends in music dictated that the issue of the show's material would be a sticky problem, particularly with the younger cast members. As always, Welk would have the last word, although he admittedly could not explain *why* a song was right or wrong for the show; he would, as he once said, "know in my bones when it's right, but I can't tell you why. It's instinctive with me."

Those pressures mounted and by show time, Welk was often seen shaking with fatigue, unsure whether he would be able to go on. Yet, when he dressed and walked on stage, the magic was always unmistakably there.

"He wanted to quit the whole thing many, many times. He wanted to leave it up to Myron or George Cates to do it and I said, 'Lawrence, there's only one *person who can stand up there. Nobody else can do it. I don't know what you're going to do, but you're stuck.'"*

—WALLY STANARD, technical director

Joe Feeney.
(Courtesy George Thow Collection)

Welk's dedication to perfection paid off less than one month after the initial September 9 broadcast. The ratings had increased by 4 million to an amazing 10.25 million homes, calculated to equal in excess of thirty-six million viewers. "The Lawrence Welk Show" proved to the public and to those within the broadcasting industry that it had not lost a bit of its luster—or drawing power. Lawrence Welk had played the odds and won, and his fans rejoiced that he was back on top.

As the ratings continued to climb, the Welk production staff planned a lavish remote program to be taped entirely on location in Hawaii in July 1972, the first of its kind for the series. It was so successful and the ratings were such that Welk half-jokingly contemplated a similar excursion to Alaska.

Unfortunately, the spectacular Hawaii remote taping was soon marred by a permeating sense of apathy when they returned home. Perhaps it was a natural reaction to the end of the tremendous pressures to make the first syndication season a smash, but for whatever reasons, Welk called this period, "when I realized what was happening, the most profoundly disturbing discovery of my lifetime." Welk even admitted that he was as guilty of slacking off as everyone else.

This lack of enthusiasm and concentration resulted in a rather lackluster final production and was mirrored by a drop in the ratings. Further adding to the problems, Welk had to ignore viewer letters requesting more band numbers when the musicians claimed they did not have adequate rehearsal time.

The result of Welk's growing anguish, anger, and frustration was a summit meeting with George Cates, Myron Floren, music arrangers Curt Ramsey and Joe Rizzo, Ted Lennon, Jack Imel, George Thow, and Welk's secretary, Lois Lamont. After stating his views on the deterioration of morale, Welk concluded by saying with great emotion that if all concerned refused to do their very best he would simply give up the show immediately. He reasoned he would rather do one or two good specials each year than a second-rate show each week, not unlike the argument he used to ABC President Thomas Moore when he insisted his program be broadcast in color and not black and white.

Myron Floren views part of the problem as being the great expansion of the Welk empire. "I think one of the biggest changes was the transition from a small country band for Lawrence into a multifaceted company where there was music publishing, real estate, and all these other things. There was so much money coming in that they had to do something with it, so they built buildings."

Floren adds, "I think the change from a close-knit group to an overpowering company was the most noticeable change. Eventually, the personalities weren't that important any more. Then we got so many personalities after a while that I was one of the lucky ones, to be there from the beginning. I was more or less established before the young ones came."

Costumer Rose Weiss observes, "The younger people hadn't even *heard* of half the music we were doing. It was probably very frustrating to them not to have been able to do the things they felt they should have been doing [compared to] what they had to do to be on the show. They lost sight of the fact that they wouldn't have made it at all if it hadn't been for the showcase they were on."

The meeting with Welk and his staff seemed to break the spell of prevailing lethargy and soon the show was, to Welk's mind, back on the track and better than ever. Welk concluded that when everyone realized they might all lose the show, the sense of unity

Another Welk birthday celebration. (Courtesy Don Keck)

Larry Hooper with Gail, Sandi, and Mary Lou.
(Courtesy Don Keck)

that had been missing reappeared and the Musical Family worked harder than ever before to ensure the show's success.

In March 1973, Lawrence Welk turned seventy years of age and was toasted at a two-week-early surprise party arranged by his old friend and loyal sponsor Matty Rosenhaus. The highlight and most emotional moment of the evening was the unannounced appearance of Larry Hooper, who had undergone extremely critical open-heart surgery more than once, which was followed by severe complications; for over a year, Larry had been unable to speak due to scar tissue that had formed on and around his vocal chords. Twice he almost lost his life. Nevertheless, Larry Hooper walked to the microphone and when Lawrence joined him on stage he announced that his recovery was complete and

he would be able to return to "The Lawrence Welk Show" that coming fall.

What was not known at the time, according to Rose Weiss, is that "when Larry Hooper got ill, Lawrence took care of *everything*, even though Larry was in the hospital for several years." Rose adds, "Whoever needed help got it."

Photographer Don Keck confirms this. "Lawrence could be very kind. One time he came to me on the stage just before we took a summer break. At that time, he had a house in Palm Springs and he said, 'You look tired. You need a break. You go to my secretary and get the keys to my place in Palm Springs. I want you down there for a week.' We got down there and the refrigerator was completely stocked, we had a swimming pool and the place all to ourselves."

Associate director Ron Bacon had a similar experience. "I got sick one time and we were at a prerecord and I just collapsed. Overwork, I guess. Lawrence wasn't there, but the very next day he phoned my home personally and asked how I was doing. He suggested that I go to Palm Springs and stay at his home until I recovered. I thought that was a kind of remarkable sensitivity."

Bacon adds, "Lawrence Welk is a very compassionate man. He got a lot of flack from people because he was a tough boss. He demanded a lot from his people, but they were loyal. They worked without contracts and stuck around."

This exceptional personal concern extended throughout the Musical Family. Myron Floren recalls a time when he was hospitalized for a life-threatening infection: "About a week before Christmas, Berdyne, my wife, and I were talking in my hospital room when we heard a lot of noise in the hallway. In walked Tanya and Larry, Guy and Ralna, and Clay and Salli, dragging a Christmas tree with ornaments and decorations!"

Norma, Ralna, Cissy, and daughter-in-law Tanya with Lawrence. (Courtesy George Thow Collection)

108

Welk was also protective of his musicians, keeping close tabs on them, making sure their conduct was above board and professional—which to him meant the absence of drugs and liquor. Rose Weiss states, "I don't think the guys in the band ever really had a tough time of it with Lawrence, unless they were drinking. If anybody was drinking, that would really be a problem."

Technical director Wally Stanard reveals, "Lawrence was a rather naive person and didn't know that guys might be on any kind of dope or booze if they weren't reliable or didn't play right. He finally asked one fellow what his problem was. The guy said, 'Well, Lawrence, I've got a monkey on my back.' And Lawrence says, 'That's alright, Bob Lido loves animals! He'll take care of him!'"

Reflecting on "The Lawrence Welk Show" at its best, Victor P. Hass reviewed the show in the *Omaha World Herald* and liked it, perhaps to his own surprise. "Lawrence Welk had a program the other Saturday evening that he called 'Nostalgia.' It was filled with lovely long-ago tunes sung by beautiful women and handsome young men, well-scrubbed, their hair neat and tidy. They made a pleasing appearance, they seemed to take pleasure in their work and the results of their efforts were entirely agreeable. It was an hour of melody that must have carried many a listener back to a time when life seemed simple, more relaxed, more liveable. I thought as I listened that Welk, for all his corny comments, is an uncommonly astute program planner because he echoed the ache in many hearts and minds these days, the longing, half-expressed, half-felt, for something better than the bash and smash, the predatoriness, the scruffiness of so much of life today. I thought, too, of Peter Citron's remark in a review that 'Welk sounded better all the time' after the ear-shattering experience of a rock concert that left him literally deafened by the assault on his ear drums."

Ron Bacon offers his analysis of why "The Lawrence Welk Show" was so good—and so popular. "Lawrence had a way of taking

"Everything he did on the show, you could hum along or sing along to, for the most part. There was never a time when you'd want to turn it off, saying, 'Gee, that sounds terrible!' It was danceable. I know a lot of people that danced at home, watching."

—NORMA ZIMMER

something very simple and making it have *excitement*, which was felt by the audience. A lot of it had to do with keeping the performers right on edge right up to curtain time and running the show pretty much like a live show, not interrupting it for a lot of technical adjustments; then the performers are able to focus their energy. I think that's the secret—it's very hard to catch the essence of a live concert on stage on television. When you get the technical things right, quite often the performance fails. Welk always kept us focused on what he knew so well, which was the show business aspect, maintaining that high level of energy on stage. Other shows I worked on didn't come off with the same energy or excitement that "The Lawrence Welk Show" did."

"In 1973, my wife of twenty-six years had passed away and I was in a deep depression and Lawrence sort of felt that. He said, 'What are you going to do this summer?' I said that I really had nothing in particular to do. He said, 'It's getting hard for me to do the show in Tahoe. Why don't you come up and direct the show up there?' I conducted the show and it got a very big hand. After the show he said, 'Look what a mistake we've made! You should do this more often.' So I would do one big number on the show and conduct all the music off. After that, I was on television [doing the same] every show."

—GEORGE CATES

*"Lovely tunes sung by beautiful women and
handsome young men . . ."* (Courtesy Don Keck)

(Courtesy George Thow Collection)

Lawrence with Henry Cuesta.
(Courtesy George Thow Collection)

The mid to late 1970s was a relatively tranquil period for "The Lawrence Welk Show." There were several talented additions to the cast, a brief but troublesome studio change from ABC to CBS, and two departures from the Musical Family. (As was the case in 1969 with Jo Ann Castle and Natalie Nevins, one was friendly and the other abrupt and highly publicized.) The touring version of the television program proved as much of a draw as ever and albums of Welk's band and his solo artists were consistently strong sellers.

During this period, music arranger Bob Ballard, band member Henry Cuesta, and singers Tom Netherton, Kathie Sullivan, and Ava Barber joined the program; they would all remain through its final days on the air.

Myron Floren has cited Bob Ballard as "one of the finest musical arrangers I know." While Ballard had worked with Floren and Welk in years past, it was not until 1973 that he became a permanent member of the show, having previously arranged music for Freddy Martin and Ray Coniff, among others.

Welk discovered country music chanteuse Ava Barber on a golf outing in Nashville, Tennessee. Welk had been so impressed with an audition tape she sent him that he called her personally and asked that she sing for him when he had occasion to be in Nashville for a golf tournament. Ava followed Lawrence around the golf course while her husband Roger Sullivan played a tape on a portable cassette recorder of Ava singing.

Roger Sullivan also took advantage of Ava's audition by conducting one for himself—playing a cassette of his own drum solos for Welk, and was also made a member of Welk's Musical Family.

Welk found Tom Netherton in Bismark, North Dakota, through the intervention of some friends who thought Tom would be perfect for his show. Welk was most impressed with the clean-cut singer, saying, "He was one of the most handsome young fellows I'd ever seen, and he had a personality to match. He had a big Robert Goulet–type voice and when I had him sing for our board [they were] absolutely bowled over by him."

Ava Barber. (Courtesy George Thow Collection)

Tom Netherton.
(Courtesy Don Keck)

113

An interesting footnote to Tom's story is the fact that it was Myron Floren who saw Tom first in Fargo, North Dakota, when Myron was making a personal appearance there. Tom approached Myron and told him that he wanted to sing with him in hopes of landing an appearance on "The Lawrence Welk Show." Floren was sold on the young man's talent and also on the impact Tom would have on Welk's female audience. Myron, however, thought that such a recommendation would have more weight coming from someone other than a band member. By coincidence, Tom had just appeared in a play in Mecora, North Carolina, in a theater run by an old friend of Welk's. Myron suggested that this friend, Harold Schaffer, write a letter praising young Netherton to Lawrence directly. The plan worked, and Tom was on "The Lawrence Welk Show" in a matter of a few months.

Kathie Sullivan met Welk when the band appeared in Madison, Wisconsin, for a concert. Kathie was assigned to escort Welk to various television interviews and appointments throughout the day, these duties bestowed upon her when she earlier had been crowned Madison's "Champagne Lady." Welk was so enchanted with the "purity and brilliance of her voice" that when she sang "My Bill" for him in his limousine Lawrence asked her to join his television cast before even leaving town. Myron Floren deemed Kathie "the perfect lady on our show. She also has a fine sense of humor and in many personal appearances gets a lot of laughs with her antics."

In 1976, Welk's drummer (and second cousin) Johnny Klein was forced to leave the band due to a painful ulcer. When Johnny was offered the post of musical librarian by Welk, the difficult spot of drummer was open and no one knew who could fill it; then, according to Welk, "the Good Lord took a hand in things and Paul Humphrey walked into my life. He is one of the super drummers in the business."

By 1978, Welk's Musical Family included the following exceptional musicians: Joe Livoti and Bob Lido (violin); Harry Hyams (viola); brass section members Mickey McMahon, Laroon Holt, Charlie Parlato, and Johnny Zell; trombonists Don Staples, Kenny Trimble, Bob Havens, and Barney Liddell; reed section members Dave Edwards, Bob Davis, and Russ Klein; rhythm section members Paul Humphrey (drums), guitarist Neil Levang, string/bass/bass guitar/tuba player Richard Maloof, keyboard artist/arranger Bob Smale; arrangers Bob Ballard, Joe Rizzo, and Curt Ramsey; assistant director Doug Smart (who in 1979 was replaced by cameraman Jim Balden); and, of course, George Thow, Chuck Koon, Roselle Friedland, Rose Weiss, Jim Hobson, George Cates, and many of the show's original ABC crew members.

"Funny thing, when we started out on KTLA a lot of people around town were calling it a Mickey Mouse band, a corny band, and all that, but at the end, there were a lot of people saying, 'Hey, if there's ever an opening, let me know!' It was a great band."

—DICK DALE

Welk's only female Champagne Music Maker chose to leave "The Lawrence Welk Show" in 1978. "It was a very hard decision to make," admits cellist Charlotte Harris. "I felt part of the group. In fact, I still do. I had three children and of course they were used to my traveling all the time all those years. I had gotten married again about a year or so before I left [to Norton Buck] and I thought it was the best thing to do, not to do a lot of traveling when I first got married." Charlotte further reveals, "At that time we all felt that the band might not go on that much longer

Kathie Sullivan and Lawrence.
(Courtesy George Thow Collection)

Lawrence and Barney Liddell.
(Courtesy George Thow Collection)

*Toasting Lawrence on his seventy-fifth birthday,
still going strong.* (Courtesy George Thow Collection)

anyway. We felt that Lawrence was getting older and every year we wondered if it was going to be renewed. When you get up close to your eighties, you get tired of working."

Although insiders may well have wondered how long Welk could keep up his television program and personal appearances, he continued to do so with incredible energy. Cameraman Mike Freedman recalls that on Welk's 1982 concert tour, "It seemed that Lawrence had more energy than *I* did. In New Orleans, he was full of vitality. Try to understand, the man was near eighty, yet he flew with the band members, he sat with them, and he was always alert with people out in the audience."

Myron Floren adds, "Lawrence believed in working most of the time. For eighteen years, we went up to Tahoe and played two shows a night, seven days a week. That was our vacation! I think he enjoyed the music so much that there was probably nothing else that really turned him on like the music business. Lawrence was afraid that if he laid off for a week people would forget him."

"Lawrence called me 'one of those women's ad-libbers.'"

—CISSY KING

Being consistently tardy for television and concert rehearsals and appearances triggered the notorious firing of Cissy King in October 1978.

Cissy was well aware of her reputation for being late and knew how deeply it upset Welk. As Dick Dale remarks, "The first date she had with the band, she missed the plane to Albuquerque, which was her hometown. I love Cissy. She's a great gal, but that's just the way she is."

"I walked into Lawrence's office," recalls Cissy, "and he said, 'I'm going to have to fire

you.' I could tell that he was serious. I said, 'Lawrence, is there something I've done to upset you? Have I embarrassed you, or is there anything other than being late?' He said, 'No, I just have to do it.'"

Cissy admits, "I was always late for rehearsals. Twice on the road I had some horrible situation where I missed an airplane twice." In that confrontation with Welk in his office that afternoon, "Lawrence addressed that. I didn't tell anybody that day [of being fired]. I just did my job and the next morning I got a call from Sam Lutz who said, 'I just want to confirm that you have been released from the show.'"

Cissy, however, doubts that Lawrence Welk himself actually made the final decision to drop her from the cast. "Lawrence made the comment to Jim Hobson, 'I just fired Cissy King and I don't know why,'" states Cissy, who concludes, "which says to me, it really wasn't his idea.

"The next week, I came back and did the show. Bobby and I did a dance step that was one of the first dances we had done together and it turned out to be the last dance that we did together on the show. At the end of the show, Lawrence always danced with somebody and quite often it was me. I danced with him because I knew it was probably my last time. He said, 'You've been so lovely, and I would like for it to be this way all the time.' I made an appointment with Lawrence for the next Monday night to talk with him. I requested to chat with him because I figured after that next night I was officially terminated so I wanted to clear things up while I was still working for him."

At their meeting that Monday evening (the day before the next taping), Welk made a highly unusual offer of a second chance by retracting his "final word," which would have allowed Cissy King to return as Bobby's dance partner both on television and in all personal appearances.

Cissy, however, refused Welk's invitation to rejoin his Musical Family because, as Cissy says, "Lawrence was making certain

Cissy: "At the end of the show, Lawrence always danced
with somebody and quite often it was me."
(Courtesy George Thow Collection)

'conditions' which were unacceptable." By refusing those terms, Cissy states, "I was giving up everything *but* my integrity." Cissy recalls, though, that this last conversation did not end bitterly and remembers that Welk concluded the meeting by saying, "You've always been somebody that I could count on and you've always been a trouper and I have nothing to argue about with your professionalism."

Of the tremendous amount of publicity that surrounded this incident Cissy says, "It wasn't my choice to leave the show and it wasn't okay with me for him to tell the press that I chose to leave, making it all fine and dandy with a bow on top."

Cissy King harbors no ill feelings towards Lawrence Welk, explaining, "Lawrence was *not* a dictator. He's a terrific, sweet man who has a terrifically strong will. I respected that in him. Also, he's a warm, fun, practical-joking, darling man. He was actually always wonderful to me."

"Cissy got let go in October," remembers Bobby Burgess. "Fortunately for me, Barbara stepped right in and I finished out the season with her."

Barbara Boylan Dixon agreed to come out of retirement to reunite with her former partner "until Bobby could find somebody else," says Barbara, who, in comparing the "new" taping format to the sometimes disastrous live broadcasts, concluded, "They had it so *easy*, taping it!" Yet tape did not always offer complete assurance that an accident might not happen, as Barbara discovered. "I was a nervous wreck. It was my sister's wedding that night and we had to hurry as soon as we were finished with the show to get to the wedding. My heel caught in my petticoat and I went right down on my face!"

Barbara's return to "The Lawrence Welk Show" was a happy one, but it in no way rekindled her desire for a full-time show business career. "I enjoyed it, but times had changed and I realized that I had made the right decision. I have a super family, I've been married for sixteen years and have so much to be thankful for . . . two wonderful children and a great husband."

And what of yet another Bobby Burgess/ Barbara Boylan reunion?

"I talked to Bobby not long ago," confesses Barbara, "and he said, 'Stay in shape—I don't know when I might need you!' He knows that he can always count on me. We still are really close friends."

Knowing that Barbara's return was only a temporary one, Bobby Burgess was under pressure to find the right woman for his new dancing partner. Bobby observes, "I've only had three partners in twenty-two years, that's pretty good really," adding wryly, "Think of all the partners that Fred Astaire has had!" He also felt that working with another partner was creatively rewarding. "Every time I changed a partner, I felt I would grow. I would combine my style with her style."

Keeping in mind the reason for Cissy King's firing, Bobby was adamant on one point: "I was looking for a gal who was *married*. I thought if I could get someone who was married, maybe her *husband* could get her there on time!" he joked.

Bobby contacted a friend who was the owner of an out-of-town dance studio where a dancer by the name of Elaine Niverson was supervisor; Bobby was told Elaine was also an excellent dancer and had a dynamic personality.

Elaine then took a plane in Los Angeles to audition for Bobby. "I picked her up at the LAX airport with my wife in the car. Elaine got off the plane and she had a big hat on, carrying a big suitcase. She *looked* like someone coming to Hollywood. It was a great mental picture. She got into the car and we went over to CBS to audition her. Every time we'd do something different, I'd look over my shoulder at my wife, and we'd both nod. I had Elaine tap dance, sing, and do jazz."

Bobby remembers the first meeting between Elaine and Lawrence Welk: "He danced with Elaine and really liked her. He said, 'It's great to dance with her. She lets me lead!' He always liked that."

What was fun the last three or four years is that I got to direct my own dances. I would write down the camera angles I wanted and, doing my own steps, I knew what would look best. It was fun. I enjoyed the show all the way through. Lawrence and I always had a great rapport. We were really good friends from the very beginning till the end. I guess that's why I was so happy doing it. It was exactly what I wanted to do."

—**BOBBY BURGESS**

Barbara's return was marked by a special waltz with Lawrence. (Courtesy George Thow Collection)

Bobby and his latest dancing partner, Elaine Niverson. (Courtesy George Thow Collection)

The reason that Bobby Burgess drove Elaine Niverson over to the CBS studios was due to a temporary two-year taping location change. The move was necessitated because ABC was enjoying a boom in television pilot production and needed Studio E on a full-time basis and, as a result, "The Lawrence Welk Show" lost its berth to make room for ABC network programs that had priority over studio rental for a syndicated series. Welk then contracted with CBS to rent studio space at Television City in Hollywood, a move that would cause many problems and

irritations. Scenery had to be constructed at ABC, set designer Charles Koon recalls, and then had to be "trucked over to CBS"; wardrobe manager Rose Weiss had similar problems with costumes.

Relying on a new crew unfamiliar with the long-established methods of smoothly producing a first-class Welk program was also a great hardship. Rudy Horvatich recalls that producer-director Jim Hobson "knew the ABC crew so well that sometimes there was no reason for a meeting, because everyone already knew what was supposed to happen and how it should happen. It was a meeting of the minds without the meeting. Then, to have to leave that and go to a strange studio and a strange crew that had to be trained again, well, it was pretty hard to take. Jim Hobson commented so many times on his unhappiness."

During an ABC strike that occurred at the time Welk was beginning the migration over to CBS, former videotape operator Wally Stanard (who would rejoin the show in 1979 as technical director when it returned to ABC) offered as a favor to assist Hobson in setting up shop at CBS. Hobson gratefully accepted the offer by Stanard, who quickly determined that the CBS studio assigned to them was ill-equipped for the likes of "The Lawrence Welk Show," with improper lighting and a much smaller stage than they had been using at ABC.

As a result of those deficiencies, George Cates says of the CBS days, "The look was entirely different." Happily, ABC contacted the Welk offices after two seasons when their heavy production schedule had abated and offered "The Lawrence Welk Show" its original location, Studio E. Welk was ecstatic at their return to ABC and, as Rudy Horvatich recalls, Lawrence was "hugging everybody," for he was able to regroup most of the original ABC crew that had been for so many years such a vital part of the program's feeling of unity—and its polish.

Lawrence Welk continued providing polish to his often inexperienced talent discoveries by means of what he called his Youth Opportunity Plan (also known as the Family Plan), which began unofficially with the Lennon Sisters in 1955.

Welk devised three distinct parts of his system. The first is vocational training, supplied by the seasoned veterans of "The Lawrence Welk Show." The second phase is personality and character training, whereby the older and younger members of the show are most generous in their willingness to help new talent, in addition to setting an example with their own complete professionalism. The

final area of the Family Plan centers around financial rewards—gifts taking the form of profit-sharing, bonuses for exceptional job performance, or items that may address a personal need such as college scholarships, a television set, or even a mortgage payment.

The last performers to benefit from the Youth Opportunity Program by appearances on "The Lawrence Welk Show" proved that the Maestro had lost none of his unerring sense of show business and crowd-pleasing potential.

Joining the series in its final years (1977–1982) were the Semonski Sisters, the Otwell Twins, the Aldridge Sisters, and Joey Schmidt.

Diane, Donna, Jo Anne, Valerie, Audrey, and Michelle Semonski made their debut on "The Lawrence Welk Show" in 1977 and the girls (with the exception of the eldest, Diane, who left to pursue a songwriting career) remained for three and a half years. Welk saw in them the potential of the Lennon Sisters, despite their lack of experience.

The Semonski Sisters.
(Courtesy George Thow Collection)

Lawrence expresses his delight with his waltz partner, Michelle Semonski.
(Courtesy George Thow Collection)

In 1976, Welk told Dwight Whitney of *TV Guide* how he discovered the Semonski Sisters. "I was in Florida playing a golf tournament when I spotted them. Six little Polish girls from New Jersey. They were terrible, just terrible. Somebody had taught them all wrong. But I saw potential there. I moved them out to my mobile-home-park-restaurant in Escondido and made the older ones singing hostesses. That would give us time to work."

During the *TV Guide* interview, the Semonski Sisters burst into Welk's dressing room and sang for them. Whitney later observed, "They may have been 'terrible' once, but today they look, and sound and feel exactly like the Lennon Sisters except that there are more of them. The littlest and most beguiling, Michelle, is even younger than Janet Lennon, the littlest and most beguiling Lennon, was the year she started. Lawrence can see it now, a never-ending supply of Lennons and Semonskis strung out into a musical eternity. Already they are established members of the 'family.'"

Welk met Sheila and Sherry Aldridge when his band played in Nashville, Tennessee, in 1977. During the performance, Welk journeyed briefly into the audience to see friends and there met two girls, both dressed alike in white suits, who tugged at the back of his jacket. They revealed to him that they very much wanted to appear on his program and also that they had already sent an audition tape to the Welk office. Welk asked the girls to sing for him backstage after the performance and reacted favorably; unfortunately, he had no openings on the show but suggested they contact him when they at some point visited Los Angeles.

Sheila and Sherry just about beat Welk back home to Hollywood when they arrived at his office the following Monday morning. They sang another number, but Welk again stated he had no spots open on the show, adding they also needed more work on their act. Undaunted, the Aldridge Sisters returned to Knoxville and repeated the exact same scene in Welk's office two months later. At that time, Welk remarked that while he still had no room for the girls on his show, he did notice improvement in their performance. Once again, the young women returned home even more determined to improve enough to get a spot on "The Lawrence Welk Show."

What finally tipped the scales in the Aldridges' favor was Tanya Falan Welk's decision to leave the show in July 1977, when by chance the Aldridges had for a third time returned to see Welk in his office. At that moment, Tanya's departure left a guest spot opening on the next show and the girls clinched Welk's decision to take a chance on them with a wonderful rendition of "All I Have to Do Is Dream." Welk was convinced of their vast improvement and the girls also won over the production staff when they auditioned for them. The Aldridge Sisters were set to make their television debut on the premiere show of the 1977 season, which was taped that August. Once again, fan mail that flooded the Welk offices in the Aldridge Sis-

ters' favor led to their becoming regular members of the Musical Family.

Lawrence Welk was faced with a wonderful dilemma in that at the same time, he had discovered another sensational singing team, Roger and David Otwell, who were twenty-year-old twin brothers. The Otwells lived in a small town called Tulia in Texas, and it was from there that a relative sent a letter and audition tape of the boys to Lawrence Welk. Welk was charmed instantly by the young men and in September 1977 invited them also to make their television debut on "The Lawrence Welk Show."

Tulia, Texas, was so excited by the Welk invitation to the hometown boys that the residents raised three hundred dollars for Roger and David to use in their travels to Los Angeles. Lawrence arranged for the twins to stay in his Champagne Towers and on their arrival that first night, he and wife Fern visited with the boys.

Welk's audience was as taken with the Otwell Twins as they were with the Aldridge Sisters, which created a peculiar problem for him—he had two good new acts, but only one spot open each week. George Cates devised the perfect solution by blending together the voices of Shelia, Sherry, David, and Roger in one act. When the four tried this harmony it excited Welk as much as it did his viewers.

It was not, however, a smooth transition initially. The Aldridge Sisters and the Otwell Twins had quite understandable reservations about performing together, afraid that each duo would lose its separate identity as an individual act. Billing them as "The Aldridge Sisters and the Otwell Twins" was the immediate solution, but the four young performers were still not at all happy with the pairing. This discontent prompted a "family meeting" among Lawrence, Shelia, Sherry, David, and Roger. Welk advised them that the future held great rewards for all of them due to the national exposure they were enjoying on his show, which would lead to personal appearances, recording contracts, and more.

*Tanya Falan Welk dances with her
father-in-law at the end of a taping.*
(Courtesy George Thow Collection)

126

The Aldridge Sisters and the Otwell Twins.
(Courtesy George Thow Collection)

Though the meeting went well, what finally convinced the Otwells and the Aldridges was their first public appearances together at Harrah's in Lake Tahoe, where Welk and company were performing on their annual three-week stay there. This new act was so well-received that it convinced everyone that the combination was a success and that, once again, Lawrence Welk was correct in his show business instinct.

The last addition to "The Lawrence Welk Show" was blond accordion player Joey Schmidt from Napoleon, North Dakota. His virtuoso playing belied his young age and Myron Floren took particular delight in "working up" new accordion duets à la "Dueling Banjos."

Of those final additions to "The Lawrence Welk Show" family, Myron Floren observes, "It was unfortunate that we went off the air, for the younger people that joined us later in the show, because they weren't there long enough to have formed any kind of faithful following."

Why *did* "The Lawrence Welk Show" end in 1982 in light of its "faithful following"?

One of the factors, believes Rose Weiss, is that "the family wanted Lawrence to relax and not go on any more," since he had reached the age of seventy-nine. Rudy Horvatich feels Welk was "very sad" about the show ending. "He wanted to go on and on," says Rudy. "His family had a part to play in it. They felt he should take it easier. They worked it out so that he could take a few years off. Whatever enjoyment he had was in the fact that he was on the air and that his fans were there. He'd stay and write autographs as long as they wanted him to."

George Cates addresses a less personal aspect surrounding the show's demise, stating that the primary reason "The Lawrence Welk Show" went off the air was due to changing trends in broadcasting—and television management.

"We never had a problem with sponsors," states Cates. "They knew that our audience had the demographics for them. We were finding that the young station managers were coming in [and they] wanted to give up the show." As a result, concludes Cates, "Larry Welk, Jr., who is head of the firm, decided they wouldn't want to see the show gradually go. It was better to go out at the top of the heap."

Dick Dale recalls one station manager who illustrated George Cates's remarks. "There was one guy in Texas, a young guy who did not like the show. He said, 'I don't give a damn if it's number *one*, it's *not* going to be on my station!' If you have people like that, it'll cut your market down."

The final taping made for a sad and very emotional evening. As Norma Zimmer recalls, "There was hardly a dry eye during the last number we sang, knowing it was the last. When Jimmy [Roberts] and I did our last duet—I think it was 'Whispering Hope'—it was so hard for me not to cry."

Of "The Lawrence Welk Show" ending its television reign, Norma says, "I was really disappointed. I think it was the end of an era. People are still hoping that it comes back on. I think it could have gone on for a few more years."

The Champagne Lady is critical of those "young station managers" who chose not to continue carrying the show despite its strong ratings. "We had the sponsors and the audience, so we have to blame the stations. They didn't want that wholesome program." Norma concludes, "It isn't what the people want, it's what the stations want to present."

Welk's television company seems to mourn the passing of the show as much as the general public. Rose Weiss says of the decision to cease production, "It was very sad. In the final analysis, when they were told the show was ending, they were all sorry to see it happen."

Dick Dale credits Lawrence Welk with the genius of sustaining the show for as long as he did. "Lawrence kept it together. He could have shut the whole thing down years before. He had enough money. But he liked to work and said he was doing it for his 'musical chil-

Norma Zimmer and Jim Roberts. (Courtesy
George Thow Collection)

dren.' I don't know if that's true or not, but I'm grateful that he did. He kept my career going." Dick also readily admits he still misses "The Lawrence Welk Show." "You can't do something for thirty-two years and just say, okay, it's all over, I'm happy. I'm not unhappy, but you sure miss it. I think I'm singing better. I had a guy come up to me and say, 'I didn't think you could talk.' I said, 'Actually, I've been doing it for years!'"

Dick adds, "Lawrence was very good to me. I got to work with some of the greatest musicians in the world. Through the years, the band just got bigger and better. At the end, it was a great band. I am very, very fortunate."

Myron Floren is clear on the reasons "The Lawrence Welk Show" became an institution in this country. "We were kind of an island in the middle of a lot of high-priced entertainment. I think people used to look on us more like the neighbors next door, who were able to sing or play an instrument or perform in some way. It was a little different than the hyped-up Hollywood product that you got in most places. We brought our audience entertainment that was happy. There were no off-color jokes or innuendos but just a good, clean, wholesome show from people who looked like they could be your next-door neighbors."

Joe Feeney serenades his ladies.
(Courtesy Don Keck)

Norma, Gail, Mary Lou, Tanya, Anacani, Cissy,
Ralna, and Sandi.
(Courtesy George Thow Collection)

130

Rudy Horvatich says of the show, "It really *was* a family affair. I'm sorry we don't have that any more today. I think it's a great big loss to our country not having Lawrence Welk on the air." Set designer Chuck Koon adds, "All shows have to end, but I was hoping it would go a few more years. Everywhere I go, people talk about it like it was still on."

In Bob Ralston's estimation, "The Lawrence Welk Show" "had the largest number of loyal viewers of any show ever. I really believe there were millions of people who if they didn't watch any other television show would stay home Saturday night or whatever night the show was on."

"Lawrence knew his audience so well," says Ron Bacon. "I've seen him stand on stage in front of an audience playing his accordion so badly you can't believe it, hitting one clam after another but smiling and enjoying it so much the audience would stand and give him an ovation. Because it was done

(Courtesy George Thow Collection)

with such flair and style and confidence. There's something to be learned by that."

Bacon continues, "The secret to his show was that it had variety and pacing. There were times when he had the big band playing and other times it was very simple. He did not overpower you with one gigantic arrangement after another. I learned quickly that Lawrence had an intuitive sense about what he was doing and what was right for that show. I think most of the people associated with the show had a good understanding of this." Ron Bacon concludes, "Lawrence Welk is one of those people who is the center of gravity for this country. It was a time in history we will never have again."

History did repeat itself to bittersweet effect when Welk and His Champagne Music Makers—and most of the television regulars—departed on what to date is Welk's final personal appearance tour, just two months after "The Lawrence Welk Show" ended.

Veteran cameraman Mike Freedman coproduced and directed the television documentary of that 1982 tour, as Jim Hobson had to bow out of the assignment due to medical reasons. That experience provided Freedman with "many great moments." He states, "There has never been anybody I've known as a performer who has been a finer human being than Mr. Welk. I consider him to be a great man."

Jim Balden was coproducer of the documentary, resuming his association with the Welk show that began in its early days when he began as a page, was promoted to crane camera operator, and then to full-time cameraman until the show moved to CBS. Of those days on "The Lawrence Welk Show," Balden says, "I looked forward to going to work. I was lucky that I got to do something I enjoyed." Balden remembers the 1982 tour as a highly emotional experience and one that he shall not forget.

"The final show that the entire Welk ensemble was together for was down in Concord, California. It was June 13, 1982. They had been on the road for three weeks and Concord was the final stop. I was up there for a couple of days and got the cameras arranged to put this final show on tape. After the concert, I kept the tape rolling and had the cameras on the musicians going up to Lawrence and hugging him. All these people were crying. It really was a sad, sad moment. Larry Welk was over in the wings and I had a camera on him and he was crying. There were probably three thousand people there, at least, and they stayed knowing that the final show was over. His daughter Shirley came out and gave a big speech about her father. His children have only known their father being in television or on the road."

While the 1982 Concord concert may be Lawrence Welk's last full-scale professional engagement, it by no means meant the end of his television career. Shortly after "The Lawrence Welk Show" folded, the series was repackaged for syndication as "Musical Memories with Lawrence Welk." For these rebroadcasts, Lawrence taped new openings, segment introductions, and closing remarks (known as "wraparounds") regarding each program from years past. Gone was the immaculate formal dress; instead, Welk looked quite dapper in casual sport clothes, as he was often pictured driving his golf cart on the grounds in Escondido.

The Welk empire continues to thrive, infused with the same energy that has kept Lawrence Welk active for these many years. Welk, who was chairman and president of his Teleklew Productions, has recently handed those responsibilities over to son Larry. Welk has many diversified business interests, including prime real estate holdings, music publishing companies (giving Welk the rights to nearly twenty thousand songs, as well as the ownership of the complete works of Jerome Kern), record royalties, television syndication sales, and the continued management of many of the Welk performing alumni.

In 1983 the financial publication *Forbes* examined Welk's vast empire. Roger Neal, who authored the study, observed, "Only a few show business people possess the combination of talent, good luck and the old-fashioned discipline to hold on to and capitalize on their peak-year incomes. Lawrence Welk is one of the few." While *Forbes* estimates Welk's fortune as $25 million, other sources have reported it to be as much as $100 million. When *Forbes* asked Welk about his wealth, he remarked, "Because I surround myself with people that can do the things I cannot do, I'm enjoying my success and I don't have to work at it too much any more."

Yet despite Lawrence Welk's enormous fortune, he never seems to have acquired a taste for extravagance. Rudy Horvatich says, "Lawrence comes from farm country and certainly appreciates everything he's got today. I doubt he knows how wealthy he is." Speaking of Welk and his wife, Fern, Rudy reveals, "They live so frugally. You wonder why, because at their station in life, you think they would have more help surrounding them to make it easy for them." Myron Floren remembers when in 1966 Lawrence "felt secure enough" to build his family a new home in Pacific Palisades, California: "Lawrence invited the band members up for a little housewarming. Lawrence greeted us at the massive front door, saying proudly, 'See what can happen when you just play the melody!'"

"He always kept his simple beginnings. I was never more aware of that when I would visit his home. Whenever Lawrence would leave the room he would always turn off the lights in that room. Jack Imel tells about meetings at Lawrence's house and wandering through the huge maze of hallways when Lawrence had turned off all the lights. They finally get in a room and are all sitting on the couch and Jack would decide he had to go to the bathroom and he doesn't know where the light switches are, so he fumbles down the hall with Chinese vases and stuff trying to find his way to the bathroom."

—RON BACON

A typical Welk Christmas.
(Courtesy Don Keck)

Myron Floren and his accordion are on the road more than two hundred days per year. (Courtesy George Thow Collection)

Norma Zimmer.
(Courtesy George Thow Collection)

What next for "The Lawrence Welk Show" Musical Family? In addition to the airing of the 1982 tour documentary in which they appear, new Christmas programs are planned for years ahead and the tradition of annual "Musical Family" picnics continues, always with Lawrence himself present.

Most of the show's alumni appear regularly around the country at concert and fair dates;

many performers are still managed by Welk's long-time business partner, Sam Lutz. Norma Zimmer and Myron Floren share not only a busy personal appearance schedule, but also the accomplishment of having written two excellent autobiographies: *Norma* (to which she is writing a sequel) and Myron's story *Accordion Man* (written with daughter Randee Floren). Both movingly detail the personal

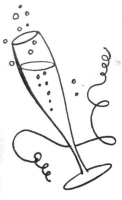

The Lennon Sisters, 1984.
(Courtesy Kathy Lennon)

hardships each have faced, but that have made their success on "The Lawrence Welk Show" that much richer. Cast members and viewers alike were deeply saddened by the deaths of Aladdin, Alice Lon, and Larry Hooper.

While Bobby Burgess continues to dance coast-to-coast with his newest partner, Elaine Niverson, Barbara Boylan Dixon remains happily in retirement. Jo Ann Castle is also a strong draw with her solo act and Cissy King tours the country with her "Two Fellows"; Charlotte Harris is now Mrs. Norton Buck and tours with him as "Charlotte and Her Cello with Norton Buck on Guitar." The Lennon Sisters, always a huge draw, are now negotiating for a new television series and have completed their joint autobiography, *Same Song, Separate Voices*.

(Courtesy George Thow Collection)

139

Another exciting television series that might well be seen in the near future is the continuation, of sorts, of Welk's Musical Family with Myron Floren at the helm, as Lawrence has been grooming Myron to do for many years. Only that program might fill the void that has remained since "The Lawrence Welk Show" went off the air in 1982.

Once, as Lawrence Welk prepared to make his entrance and the television cameras were about to roll, he paused, just as he was leaving his dressing room. "I have much to be grateful for," he reflected. "Everything a man could want in this world."

And we are all so grateful to him. Few performers have given so unselfishly and consistently for such a long period of time—a career that has spanned more than sixty years. Lawrence Welk outlasted every other bandleader on television, and every passing musical trend, and as a reward attracted an audience of more than thirty million people each week for nearly thirty years. Lawrence Welk gave his audience precisely what they wanted, and was as fiercely devoted and protective of his public as they were of him.

Lawrence Welk has always been himself—sincere, direct, a man of strong principles and one never tainted by personal scandal. Few celebrities—or few of us—could survive as well under the moral and professional codes by which he abides. As a result, he has become an institution, a show business legend, a television pioneer, a notable part of America's history, and an important part of our lives.

"The Lawrence Welk Show," sadly, will never be again, and because of that, there will be less music in our hearts.

What shall remain always are the warm, nostalgic remembrances we share of Lawrence Welk and "The Lawrence Welk Show" —which will forever be wunnerful, wunnerful.

Bibliography

Wunnerful, Wunnerful! Lawrence Welk with Bernice McGeehan (Prentice-Hall, 1971).

Ah, One, Ah Two! Lawrence Welk with Bernice McGeehan (Prentice-Hall, 1974).

My America, Your America, Lawrence Welk with Bernice McGeehan (Prentice-Hall, 1976).

This I Believe, Lawrence Welk with Bernice McGeehan (Prentice-Hall, 1979).

Lawrence Welk: An American Institution, William K. Schweinher (Nelson-Hall, 1980).

Lawrence Welk's Musical Family Album, Lawrence Welk with Bernice McGeehan (Prentice-Hall, 1977).

The Lawrence Welk Scrapbook, Susan Katz (Grosset & Dunlap, 1978).

Norma, Norma Zimmer (Tyndale House Publishers, 1976).

Accordion Man, Myron Floren and Randee Floren (Stephen Green Press, 1981).

Index

ABC Network program, 9–96
  budget for, 53
  cancellation of, 95–96
  Christmas show, first, 17, 20
  color broadcasting of, 66–67
  first, 10
  mistakes on, 71
  schedule for, 17
  taping of, 66, 68, 70–71
ABC Radio Network show, 6–7
Aldridge, Sheila, 123, 125, 128
Aldridge, Sherry, 123, 125, 128
Aldridge Sisters, 123, 125, 128
Amodeo, Orie, 23
Anacani, 99
Anderson, Lynn, 83, 84, 85
Angel, Jimmy, 49
Aronowitz, Alfred G., 98
audience
  loyalty of, 1, 3, 12, 24, 42, 64–66, 94, 140
  Welk's concern for, 12, 37, 41, 42–44, 60, 73, 140

Bailey, Norm, 23
Balden, Jim, 45, 49, 114, 132
Ballard, Bob, 112, 114
Bacon, Ron, 23, 24, 47, 68, 70, 108, 109, 135
Barber, Ava, 112, 113

Blenders, 76
bonus system, 64
Boulds, Lincoln, 3
Boylan, Barbara, 38–41, 50, 137
  joining show, 36, 40
  leaving show, 76, 78–79, 85
  returning to show, 120
bubbles and bubble machine, 17
Buck, Charlotte Harris. *See* Harris, Charlotte
Burgess, Bobby, 36, 38–41, 48, 76, 85–86, 99,
  118, 119, 120, 137

Carter, Bert, 9
Castle, Jo Ann, 29–30, 36, 50, 137
  joining show, 29
  leaving show, 92
Cates, George, 11, 12, 22, 23, 24, 33, 45, 67, 97,
  101, 106, 109, 114, 123, 125, 128
Champagne Ladies. *See* Linn, Roberta; Lon,
  Alice; Zimmer, Norma
Connolly, Dick, 58, 59
contracts, lack of written, 63–64
costumes, 51, 53, 54, 55, 101, 122
crew members, 47–50, 122–123
Cuesta, Henry, 112

Dale, Dick, 4, 7, 10, 11, 16, 17, 30, 59, 64, 99,
  114, 118, 128–129

Davis, Bob, 114
Delo, Ken, 74, 91, 99
Dixon, Barbara Boylan. *See* Boylan, Barbara
Dixon, Greg, 76
documentary of 1982 tour, television, 132–133
Dodge Motor Company (sponsor), 9, 10, 12, 28
Duncan, Arthur, 79, 91, 99

Edwards, Dave, 114

Falan, Tanya, 99
    joining show, 88, 89
    leaving show, 125
Falk, Herm, 49
Family Plan, 123
fans. *See* audience
Farrell, Gail, 99
Fedderson, Don, 9–10, 17, 67, 82, 87, 96
Feeney, Joe, 26, 33, 99, 101
fever chart, 37
Floren, Berdyne, 13, 108
Floren, Kristie, 85
Floren, Myron, 10, 12–13, 28, 40, 44, 71, 79, 83,
    96, 99, 106, 108, 112, 114, 118, 128, 129,
    133, 136, 140
Floren, Randee, 136
Flynn, Salli, 88, 91, 99
Fountain, Pete, 27
Freedman, Mike, 45, 59, 68, 118, 132, 133
Friedland, Roselle, 50, 51, 114

Gaunt, John, 10
Grant, Hank, 63
Griffiths, Brent, 91
Griffiths, Sandi Jensen, *See* Jensen, Sandi

Haines, Bob, 100
Harris, Charlotte, 36, 92, 137
    joining show, 36
    leaving show, 114
Hart, Clay, 88, 91, 99
Hart, Salli Flynn. *See* Flynn, Salli
Hass, Victor P., 109
Havens, Bob, 114
Helm, Dick, 87
Hobson, Jim, 22, 24, 45, 46, 53, 56, 68, 87, 103,
    114, 118, 122, 123, 132
Holland, Eddie, 23, 30, 45, 58, 64
Holt, Laroon, 114
Hooper, Larry "Hoopy," 11, 16–17, 99, 107
    death of, 137
    joining show, 16

Horvatich, Rudy, 30, 44, 50, 51, 71, 73, 97, 122,
    123, 125, 132, 133
Hotsy Totsy Boys, 99, 100
Hoyis, Guy, 92, 99
Hoyis, Ralna, 92, 99
Hucko, Peanuts, 99
Humphrey, Hal, 24
Humphrey, Paul, 114
Hyams, Harry, 114

Imel, Jack, 26, 99, 100, 101, 106

J. B. Williams Company (sponsor), 28, 66, 96
Jensen, Sandi, 88, 91, 99

Keck, Don, 30, 50, 51, 54, 64, 107
Kelly, Alma, 3
Kelly, George T., 3
Kennedy, Joseph P., 65, 66
King, Cissy, 40, 85–87, 90, 99, 118, 137
    firing of, 118–120
    joining show, 85
Kintner, Robert E., 10
Klein, Johnny, 23, 114
Klein, Russ, 23, 100, 114
Koon, Charles "Chuck," 17, 50, 51, 53, 54, 114,
    122, 132
KTLA television program, 7–9
Kudge, P. F., 94

Lamont, Lois, 44, 48, 106
Landsberg, Klaus, 7, 8
"Lawrence Welk and His Hotsy Totsy Boys—The
    Biggest Little Band in America," 4
Lawrence Welk Television Network, 96–97
"Lawrence Welk's Top Tunes and New Talent,"
    25, 26
Lennon, Dianne, 20, 21, 22, 79
Lennon, Janet, 20, 22, 79, 82
Lennon, Kathy, 20, 21, 22, 50, 53, 67, 71, 79, 83
Lennon, Peggy, 20, 22, 82
Lennon Sisters, 20–23, 50, 79–83, 137
    audition for, 21–22
    early career of, 20–21
    joining show, 22
    leaving show, 82, 84
    maturation of, 51, 79, 82
Lennon, Ted, 96, 106
Levang, Neil, 114
Lidell, Barney, 23, 48, 114
Lido, Bob, 11, 23, 99, 100, 114
Lincoln Boulds Orchestra, 3

Linn, Roberta (Champagne Lady), 8, 11
Little, Tiny, Jr., 11
Livoti, Joe, 99, 114
Lon, Alice (Champagne Lady), 11–12, 30–31, 137
Lutz, Sam, 7, 9, 17, 40, 67, 87, 91, 96, 136

McMahon, Mickey, 114
Maloof, Richard, 100, 114
Merrill, Buddy, 11, 23, 99
Metzger, Mary Lou, 99
Miller High Life (sponsor), 6–7
Minor, Jack, 10
Moore, Thomas W., 67, 106
Moss, Morton, 94
music style, 24, 36, 60, 64, 82, 94–95, 109, 129, 132
"Musical Memories with Lawrence Welk," 133

Neal, Roger, 133
Netherton, Thomas, 112, 113–114
Nevins, Natalie, 75, 92
Niverson, Elaine, 40, 120, 137

O'Brien, Jack, 64
"Oh Happy Day," 17
Otwell, David, 23, 125, 128
Otwell, Roger, 123, 125, 128
Otwell Twins, 123, 125, 128

Pallante, Aladdin, 11, 76, 137
Parlato, Charlie, 100, 114
pay, minimum, 64
Pearson, Maurice, 26
"Peerless Entertainers, The," 3
photographic file, 53, 54–55
Plymouth (sponsor), 25
"Plymouth Show, The," 25
Portner, Ralph, 9, 24, 27, 43
profit-sharing system, 64

radio shows, 5–7
Ralston, Bob, 3, 59–60, 84, 99, 100
Ramsey, Curt, 106, 114
ratings, 87
    drop in, 103, 105
    gain in, 12, 24, 105
record albums, 112
Renner, Fern. See Welk, Fern retirement fund, 64
Rizzo, Joe, 45, 71, 106, 114
Roberts, Jim, 10–11, 33, 99, 128

rock 'n' roll, 94–95
Rockwell, Rocky, 10
Rosenhaus, Matthew, 66, 96, 107

Sandi and Salli, 88, 91, 99
Schmidt, Joey, 123, 128
Scott, Frank, 23
Semonski, Audrey, 123–124
Semonski, Diane, 123–124
Semonski, Donna, 123–124
Semonski, Michelle, 123–124
Semonski, Valerie, 123–124
Semonski Sisters, 123–124
sets, 51, 53, 54, 55, 101, 122
Smale, Bob, 114
Smart, Doug, 114
Smith, Steve, 76
Sobel, Ed, 17, 22, 41, 45, 53,
Sparklers Quartet, 11
Standard, Wally, 31, 45, 103, 109, 123
Staples, Don, 114
station managers, and demise of show, 128
Sullivan, Kathie, 112, 114
Sullivan, Roger, 113
syndication, 96–97
    and apathy, 105–106
    ending of, 128, 129, 132
    and Hawaii remote taping, 105
    and premiere show, 100–101, 103
    and ratings, 103, 105
    repackaging for, 133
    and taping location change, 122–123
    touring version of, 112

Teleklew Productions, 53, 63, 133
television documentary, of 1982 tour, 132–133
television show. See also ABC Network Program;
    syndication
    demise of, 128, 129, 132
    first local (KTLA), 7–9
    repackaging of, 133
Thow, George "Gus," 50, 55–57, 64, 106, 114
Trimble, Kenny, 114

wages, scale, 64
Warren, Bob, 101
Weiss, Rose, 50, 51, 53, 64, 101, 106, 107, 109, 114, 122, 128
Welk, Christina (mother), 3
Welk, Fern (wife), 4–5, 133
Welk, Kevin, (grandson), 90

Welk, Lawrence
  ad-libbing by, 57
  birth of, 3
  broken English of, 9, 48, 98
  childhood of, 1, 2, 3
  childrens' births, 5
  control by, 45, 103
  creation of orchestra by, 4
  cue cards for, 57–58
  early career of, 3–7
  empire of, 63, 68, 106, 133
  final personal appearance tour of, 132–133
  grandchildren of, 90
  marriage of, 5
  personal qualities of, 1, 44, 87, 107–109, 140
  quoted, 1, 87, 100
  radio career of, 4–7
  television industry awards not given to, 24
  wealth of, 1, 133
  work ethic of, 63, 74
Welk, Lawrence Leroy, Jr. (son), 5, 21, 90, 133
Welk, Lawrence III (grandson), 90
Welk, Ludwig (father), 3
Welk, Shirley (daughter), 5, 133
Welk, Tanya Falan. *See* Falan, Tanya
Whitney, Dwight, 124
Willis, Andrea, 83–85
writing, for show, 56

Youth Opportunity Plan, 123

Zell, Johnny, 114
Zimmer, Norma (Champagne Lady), 12, 18, 33–36, 42, 50, 64, 71, 84–85, 99, 109, 128, 136